TORCHBEARER OF THE REVOLUTION

TORCHBEARER
OF THE REVOLUTION

The Story of Bacon's Rebellion and Its Leader

BY THOMAS JEFFERSON WERTENBAKER

PRINCETON UNIVERSITY PRESS · PRINCETON
LONDON · HUMPHREY MILFORD, OXFORD UNIVERSITY PRESS
· 1940 ·

Copyright 1940 by Princeton University Press

Printed in the United States of America
by Princeton University Press, Princeton, New Jersey

Preface

LIFE IN THE AMERICAN COLONIES DEVELOPED A GREAT race of men, but few great individuals. The task of the settlers was to conquer a continent for civilization, not to make advances in astronomy, or physics, or medicine, nor to produce great literary works. This settler might have been a Shakespeare had he remained in England, this one a statesman, this an artist; in America he had to devote himself to the humbler tasks of making a clearing in the forest, building a cabin, fighting the Indians, planting crops, rearing a family in the wilderness. Not until the colonies had acquired wealth, built up a system of schools and colleges and developed a leisure class, did it produce men of the stamp of Benjamin Franklin and George Washington.

Nathaniel Bacon was the greatest figure of the first century of American history. And though he was born in England and lived in this country little more than two years, America can justly claim him for her own. Not only were the important events of his life crowded into the period of his stay in Virginia, but in his love of individual liberty, his self-reliance, his hatred of oppression he was at home on the American frontier and showed himself akin to the leaders of the Revolution.

This book was written in the hope that at last justice would be done to the memory of this remarkable man. Bacon died in the midst of his struggles, his followers went down to defeat and he was branded as a traitor. But a study of the records show him to have been rather a patriot, a champion of the weak, a rebel against in-

PREFACE

justice, the forerunner of Washington, Jefferson and Samuel Adams.

I wish to express my deep appreciation for the invaluable suggestions of Mr. Joseph A. Brandt and Mr. Datus C. Smith, Jr., of the Princeton University Press. I am indebted, also, to Mr. William R. Hersey, of South Harwich, Mass., and Miss Ida A. R. Wylie, of Princeton, N.J., both of whom read the manuscript.

THOMAS J. WERTENBAKER

Harwich Port, Mass.
August 6, 1940.

Contents

Preface	v
I. Seeds of Rebellion	3
II. The Squire of Henrico	39
III. The Indian Terror	69
IV. Battles on the James	103
V. Prologue to the American Revolution	141
VI. Liberty Deferred	183
Essay on Authorities	215
Index	229

CHAPTER I
SEEDS OF REBELLION

"VIRGINIA'S FOES, TO WHOM . . . JUST VENGEANCE
OWES DESERVED PLAGUES"

Seeds of Rebellion

It was a strange fate which decreed that the leader of the first American revolt against English authority should have been an Englishman who had come to the colony of Virginia only a few months before it occurred. Washington, Jefferson, Samuel Adams and others foremost in the war for independence, had been identified since youth with the cause of American freedom. Trained in those schools of political rights—the colonial Assemblies—suspicious of the royal governor, it was inevitable that they should take up the challenge of the Stamp Act, the Townshend Acts and the Boston Massacre. But Nathaniel Bacon was almost a stranger to America and to the people who were to hail him as their hero, when a century before Lexington and Concord he protested against the repressive measures of the mother country, took up arms against the royal governor, drove him from his capital, defeated his troops and stood ready to give battle to the redcoats sent over to suppress him.

Stranger still is it that this man who sacrificed his life in the cause of the poor and downtrodden, was the spoiled child of a wealthy English squire. Thomas Jefferson, Bacon's legitimate successor, although identified with the Virginia aristocracy through his mother, was descended on his father's side from the small farmer class which he idealized in his political philosophy. Bacon was an aristocrat by right of both mother and father. It has been suggested that he fell in with a group of young liberals, possibly when he was at Gray's Inn, who filled his mind with republican principles. But since the records of this famous law school went up in flames two centuries and a half ago, we are left to conjecture why this sophisticated young Englishman could so readily have been transformed into the frontier fighter and revolutionary leader of men.

Possibly Nathaniel inherited his republican leanings from the grandfather for whom he was named, who, like so many east county squires, sympathized with Parliament in the struggle with Charles I. That he and his son Thomas, Nathaniel's father, actually fought against the King is not certain, but we have proof that they were among the leaders in protesting against his policies— what they termed the many illegal taxes, the introduction of innovations and superstitions in the Church, the endeavors to subvert the fundamental laws of England and set up arbitrary and tyrannical government. The elder Nathaniel died before the younger was born, but his "horse and foot arms" which were carefully preserved in the family mansion at Friston, spoke eloquently of battles and sieges, of marches and victories for the cause of free government. And stories of Naseby or Worcester told around the table in the great dining hall may have had their repercussions two decades later on the banks of the James in far-away Virginia, when the young Suffolk squire took up arms against the despotism of Sir William Berkeley.

Save for the political leanings of his family, there was little that savored of democracy in the boy's upbringing. His father was typical of the landed gentry who ruled the English countryside in the seventeenth century as lords of the manor, owners of broad acres in fee simple, justices of the peace, patrons of the churches, members of the

House of Commons and devotees of learning and the arts. He was the polished Sir Roger de Coverley, not the boorish Squire Western. From his "chief mansion house" at Friston, with its ancient halls and its twenty fireplaces, he could look out over his fields, pastures, tenant cottages and woodlands. Among his possessions were the manors of Alderton Hall, Bovell's, Howe's, Earle Alderton and Daymes; and the lands and tenements in Hollesley, Ramsholt, Bawdsey, Shottisham, Sutton, Friston, Snape, Buxton and Sternfield. When he attended religious services in little St. Mary's at Friston, with its ancient flint tower and Norman doorway, he was received with all the deference due the patron.

As an only son, the heir to these great estates, the youthful Nathaniel was accustomed not only to the homage of the servants and tenants, but of his aunt, his sisters and perhaps even his stepmother. His own mother, Elizabeth Brooke, daughter of Sir Robert Brooke, had died when he was an infant, and his father had later married again. Though the life at Friston Hall tended to give Nathaniel an exaggerated opinion of his own importance, it was full of wholesome interest and adventure. There were books to read in the "parlor" and the "closet"; places for play in the bakehouse, the brew house, the dairy, the "mill house" and other outbuildings; there were visits to the market and fair at the nearby village of Saxmundham.

When Nathaniel was still a very small boy an event took place which was to have a profound effect on his life —his cousin, also named Nathaniel Bacon, migrated to Virginia. The son of the Reverend James Bacon, and with no large inheritance or influential position to look forward to, this young man decided to seek his fortune in what was then the land of hope. Stories had filtered back to England of how hundreds, who found the path to advancement closed to them at home, had gone to Virginia and in a very short time acquired both wealth and influence. Although the land was very fertile, it was so cheap that one could acquire a goodly estate by the outlay of a few pounds. With every acre yielding a rich harvest of tobacco which could be sold in England or Holland at from two to three pence per pound; with cattle, horses, sheep and swine so plentiful that many ran wild in the forests, with wheat and corn abundant, with every small farm boasting of its orchard, with political advancement easy and rapid, the advice, "Go west young men," was sound indeed even though it necessitated a three thousand mile voyage in the tiny vessels of the day.

Despite these many opportunities the elder Nathaniel Bacon would not have found Virginia the Utopia it was represented, had he not brought with him the chief attributes for success. He was hard working, thrifty, prudent, tactful; a man of education and good family in a land where both were at a premium. We follow him through successive steps from the poor immigrant to the highest post in the colony—small landowner, justice of York County, member of the House of Burgesses, member of the Council of State, auditor of Virginia, president of the Council, acting governor. Wealth he acquired through his marriage with Elizabeth Kingsmill, widow of William Tayloe, but he added to it by his own prudent adventures as planter, merchant and shipowner. At his death in 1691 he possessed a goodly plantation on King's Creek, real estate in Jamestown and elsewhere, large personal property and no less than forty negro slaves.

But for one man of education and social standing who came to Virginia there were scores of poor mechanics and laborers driven over by hard times in England, low wages and the difficulty in securing work. These men, since in most cases they were penniless, bartered off a few years of freedom in return for their transportation across the Atlantic. Meeting with a colonial agent in a tavern on the London river front, they would listen to his accounts of opportunities in Virginia, which seemed all the more glowing because of a few drinks of ale or rum. So they would affix their signatures, or more frequently marks, to an indenture, or contract, agreeing to serve a "master" in the colony for four years as laborers in the tobacco fields. Then followed the dangerous voyage across the ocean in cramped quarters amid crates and casks, a nightmare of seasickness, bad food, worse drink and perhaps serious illness. Upon landing in Virginia they at once began working off their terms.

At the expiration of the indentured worker's four years, if the Virginia sickness had not claimed him as one of its countless victims, he found himself a free man, with life in the colony before him. The future now depended upon his own ambition, initiative, strength and capacity for work. If his health had been undermined by illness and overwork, or if he had acquired vicious habits, or if he were lazy and shiftless he might content himself with working for wages at odd times or he might become a squatter on the frontier, sheltering himself with a tumbledown shack and living on corn meal and game. If he possessed the stuff which makes for success he might save enough money to purchase a little plantation of from fifty to a hundred acres, erect a cottage and a tobacco house, plant an orchard, lay out a vegetable garden, clear away the trees for his tobacco field, and so become a member of the yeoman class. He might in time even become a justice of the peace, or go to Jamestown to represent his county in the House of Burgesses where he would be respected as one of the colony's many self-made men.

But the small farmer class was recruited not only from indentured workers, but from Englishmen of meager means, yeomen many of them, who paid with cash the ocean fares for themselves and their families and began life as freemen immediately upon their arrival. By following one of them—Peter Bottom, let us call him—a tenant farmer of Essex, we gain an insight into the creation of the Virginia yeomanry—the intelligent, prosperous, self-respecting small farmers, who constituted the backbone of the colony.

Peter has heard much of Virginia. A friend on a neighboring manor has a son there who writes glowing accounts of his success—how he owns a farm of one hundred and fifty acres, has meat for dinner every day, enjoys fruit and vegetables in season, is erecting a small but comfortable cottage. Now Bottom labors from dawn till dark, he has to pay £5 a year for the use of his land and occasionally perform personal services for the lord of the manor, he considers himself extravagant if he tastes meat once a week, his entire yearly income is barely enough to support his wife and children, if he hunts in the nearby woods he runs the risk of arrest for poaching. Life stretches out before him as a long hard struggle, with meager rewards and little chance of eventual betterment for himself and his children.

There follow long and earnest consultations in the humble, thatched cottage where he, and his father before him, have spent their lives. With the savings of many years he has thought of purchasing a freehold nearby, a little farm of ten acres which could be made to yield a fair living. But now the letter of his friend's son turns his thoughts to Virginia. He hesitates to leave his native shire, to cut himself off from friends and relatives, to face the perils of the ocean, to begin life over again in a strange and distant land; he wonders whether he would be successful as a tobacco grower, whether he would fall a victim to the Virginia sickness. But when he realizes that his savings are sufficient not only to take his family to the colony but to purchase a farm twenty times as large as the Essex freehold, he decides to make the great venture and throw in his lot with Virginia.

A few months later Peter, with his wife and two children, stands wonderingly at the rail of a tobacco ship as it sails in between Cape Charles and Cape Henry and heads for the mouth of James River. The sight of land is welcome indeed to the weary passengers after their long voyage, even though the sandy beaches and vast forests are in marked contrast to their own Essex. As the vessel comes nearer to shore they can see clearings in the woods, with little frame cottages surrounded by tobacco fields. For the newcomers this is a supreme moment. They are looking for the first time upon the land which is to be their home, the home of their children and their grandchildren. It is the land they had dreamed of, where hard work yields rich returns, where the poor may become rich, the lowly rise to prominence.

They realize that they are no longer Englishmen in the full sense, but Virginians, who share in Virginia's prosperity or suffer with her misfortunes, who must carve their fortune from her soil, perhaps bear arms in her defense.

At Jamestown they come ashore, bringing with them their belongings—a wooden chest laden with clothes, a few pewter cups and plates, a spit, a ladle, a kitchen pot, a churn, a bolster, three hoes, two shovels, a spade, two broad axes, several saws, a grindstone, ten pounds of nails. To his surprise Peter learns that he will not have to purchase a farm since he is entitled by law to two hundred acres, fifty acres as a reward for bringing himself to the colony, fifty more for his wife and one hundred for the two children. So he walks over to the secretary's office, in the quaint little capitol, and inquires anxiously as to the location of a desirable tract. The secretary marks off two hundred acres in Henrico, above the "curles" of the James, signs and delivers his patent, and leaves him to find out for himself the exact location of his property and how to reach it.

By diligent inquiry Peter learns that his tract lies on the frontier, accessible to river boats, but entirely covered with the primeval forest growth of giant walnut trees, oaks, cypresses and cedars. He now thinks of leaving his family in one of the Jamestown ordinaries while he prepares a home for them, but the prices are so high that his funds will not permit. He is balked, also, when he seeks a laborer to assist him in the difficult tasks which confront him, for he finds that to purchase an indentured worker is beyond his means, while hired men are scarce and wages four times as great as in England. So he engages a shallop, loads his goods on board, and with his wife and children heads for the upper James. It requires several days to make the trip to Bermuda Hundred, then around the Curles, past Varina, the river becoming narrower as they go, the forests more dense, the clearings fewer, the houses more primitive.

At last they arrive at their wilderness "farm" and after unloading their belongings in the shadow of the great trees send the shallop back. Now follow weeks and months of hard work and privation. Sheltering his family under a temporary shack made of boughs and bark, Peter takes his axe and brings down one tree after another, saws the trunks into eight-foot lengths and hews them into rough beams. Unlike the pioneers of the eighteenth and nineteenth centuries, he knows nothing of log-cabin construction, so that his little cottage as it takes shape, is a rough replica of the old homestead in Essex. First the oak frame is put together with its sharply rising roof lines, then a crude wooden chimney, then the clapboards are riven and nailed to the rafters and uprights, then the doors are hung, the sliding shutters placed in the windows and the family moves in.

In most countries and ages trees have been a priceless asset, providing timber for houses, ships and the manufacture of paper, yielding pitch, tar and resin, but to the early American colonists they were often a nuisance. For Peter to clear with his axe the trees from fifteen or twenty of his two hundred acres would keep him busy for many months, while his stores of food declined and the time for laying out his crops passed. So, following the example of other frontiersmen, he cuts the bark in a ring around the trunks and leaves the trees to die. With the coming of spring he breaks the ground with his hoe and plants his tobacco, Indian corn and wheat beneath the naked outstretched limbs. Next winter, when he is not so pressed for time, he will bring down these dead monarchs of the forest, grub up the roots and give his crops greater space and sunshine.

At times, when Peter is exhausted by hard work, or when his children are ill, or when he listens to the howling of the wolves, he wonders whether he has been wise in leaving England. But then he thinks of his two hundred acres and turns his thought hopefully and doggedly to the future. With the sprouting of his grain, the ripening of the tobacco and corn, the harvesting of the crops, the curing of his Sweetscented, he fancies himself already on the road to prosperity. It is November when, hearing that a Dutch merchant ship is trading at Bermuda Hundred, he hires a shallop from his nearest neighbor and loading it with tobacco drifts down the river. He draws up alongside the Dutchman, comes aboard to haggle over the price, and finally disposes of his crop for £15. To Peter this is a princely sum, so after laying out part of it in cheap Dutch goods and part in a cow and calf, he returns rejoicing to his plantation.

We cannot follow in detail our friend through the years which follow, years full of hard work, but also of increasing prosperity. Peter opens new fields, plants an orchard, erects his tobacco house, purchases a shallop, builds fences, increases his stock of cattle, pigs and poultry, adds a new room to his cottage, secures several pieces of crude furniture, and at last, ten years after his arrival in the colony, pays £10 for the services of an indentured worker. He has won the respect of his neighbors, is a corporal in the Henrico militia, holds his head high when he goes down the river to Varina on Sundays to attend services in the little church.

There were hundreds of Peter Bottoms in pre-Restoration Virginia. Their plantations, stretching out on the banks of the James, the York, the Rappahannock and the Potomac and up the tributary creeks, supplied the bulk of the tobacco which went out to England and Holland. Almost entirely English in blood, intelligent, jealous of their rights, they formed the backbone of a homogeneous, democratic society.

It is true that an aristocracy was also emerging, men of the type of Adam Thoroughgood, George Menefie and Samuel Mathews, who filled the Council of State, were commanders of the militia and monopolized the most lucrative public offices, but they were outnumbered fifty to one by the yeomen. If a wealthy planter, Nathaniel Bacon, senior, let us say, occupied a seat in the county court, or the vestry, or in the House of Burgesses, he might find at his right hand a small farmer, at his left one who had served out his term of indenture. There was no caste system in Virginia. The poor immigrant of today became the yeoman of tomorrow; the yeoman of today the large planter of tomorrow. It was the governor, Sir William Berkeley, in an address before the assembly, who declared that hundreds of examples testified to the fact that no man was denied the opportunity to rise and acquire both property and honor.

It was a priceless asset for England as well as the colony, this democratic type of society. The tobacco yeoman made for strength—economic strength, since he was so large a producer of tobacco and so great a purchaser of English goods; military strength, since he belonged to the militia and was ever ready to battle for colony and King; political strength, since he was a staunch friend of representative government and civil rights; but above all social strength, since he typified equality of opportunity and a just division of natural resources. Well would it have been had England so shaped her laws and the policies of her governors as to foster the small farmer class, sheltering them from the encroachments of the grasping aristocracy, from the killing competition of slave labor and from unjust restrictions upon their trade. Then there would have been no Bacon's Rebellion, perhaps no American Revolution, no War between the States, no racial problem, no Solid South.

But since England was blind to the situation in the colony and gave not the slightest heed to the character of the social structure, the small farmer class was subjected to a series of unjust and unwise measures which at times threatened its very existence. When the yeomanry in 1676, under the leadership of young Bacon, struck out wildly against the oppressions of England, Charles II and his ministers were greatly surprised. But the rebellion was one of self-preservation, the vigorous protest of men driven to desperation at what seemed for the moment to be their very destruction, the transformation of Virginia from a democratic to an aristocratic society.

When Sir William Berkeley came to Virginia as governor in 1642, no one suspected that he would eventually become the archenemy of colonial democracy, since for the moment he seemed to be its greatest friend. This dashing young Cavalier, a brother of Lord John Berkeley and the staunchest of royalists, had no sooner set foot in the colony than he proved himself a friend of the people. When the Indians, under the leadership of the ancient but treacherous Opechancanough, fell upon the unsuspecting English and slaughtered them by the hundreds, it was Sir William, heedless of personal safety, who defeated them and brought a lasting peace. The memory of those early campaigns, with the youthful governor leading his men through the forests to bring fire and destruction to the Indian villages, lingered for decades even when he had become old and crabbed and tyrannical.

Nor could anyone have foreseen, when Berkeley was urging one liberal reform after another, that he would eventually forfeit the people's love and drive them into despair and rebellion. Hardly had he arrived in Virginia when he gave his assent to an act to make the Assembly, that bulwark of popular rights, the supreme court of the colony; secured the abolition of the unjust poll tax and urged a new levy "proportioning in some measure payments according to men's abilities and estates"; exempted the Burgesses from arrest during sessions of Assembly and limited and fixed the fees of the secretary's office. So grateful were the people that the Assembly made him a gift of two houses and an orchard, and paid his royal pension which had been suspended because of the English Civil War.

It was an ideal rôle which Berkeley played, the double rôle of official governor and popular leader, for it strengthened the ties of affection for England, made for prosperity and growth, and won the loyal support of the colony. Had he continued in it throughout his two long administrations, instead of changing into the petty despot whose chief aim was to build up a system of personal rule through favoritism, injustice and oppression, the people would not have turned from him to center their hopes in young Bacon. Berkeley himself seems not to have realized that a transformation was taking place in his character and conduct which was brewing a storm that would break furiously over his head. To the end he prided himself on his ability as a leader and was bitterly vexed and hurt when he found that the people's love had changed to hate and fear. The drama played out in the rebellion of 1676 was not only the drama of a wronged people striking out blindly against injustice, but of two unique personages, one the youthful, daring Bacon, the other the wilful, despotic governor, contending for the confidence of the colony.

How the unfortunate change in Berkeley came about we are forced to conjecture, since even the people of his own day could give no satisfactory explanation. It was the current opinion that the folly of his old age came from marrying a young wife. Hardly more convincing is the theory of a recent writer that he suffered from hardening of the arteries, which affected his brain, produced senile decay and made him cruel, vindictive and irritable. In 1672, William Edmundson called on Sir William to intercede for the Quakers, who were prohibited from holding meeting in the colony under pain of heavy fine. The next day a friend asked him how the governor had received him. "He was brittle and peevish," was the reply.

The friend asked if the governor called him "dog, rogue, etc."

"No," said Edmundson.

"Then you took him in his best humor, those being his usual terms when he is angry."

Though it may possibly have been ill-health which soured Sir William's temper, the change in his attitude to popular government is more readily accounted for by the English Civil War. He looked on with horror as the royal forces were defeated, the King led to his execution, his friends driven into exile and Oliver Cromwell established as Protector. It was all the result of yielding to the demands of wicked republicans, he thought, whose design from the first had been to overthrow both Church and State. So surrounding himself with a bodyguard and putting the colony in a posture of defense, he solemnly proclaimed Charles II King of England, an act which won for Virginia the title of the Old Dominion.

When, in 1652, a British fleet sailed up the James River, its decks crowded with Cromwell's veterans, its cannons pointing menacingly out at the planters' cottages, Sir William made ready to resist. The militia came pouring into Jamestown and took position on the river front, several Dutch vessels were pressed into service, filled with soldiers and moored in close to the fort. But in the end, when very liberal terms of surrender were proposed, when the militia were showing signs of defection and even

SEEDS OF REBELLION

the members of the Council advised against fighting, the governor, his soul full of bitterness, was forced to yield. But deep in his heart he must have vowed that if ever again he should become the chief executive of Virginia there should be no compromise with popular demands.

For more than seven years he waited, a private citizen of what in fact was the almost independent Republic of Virginia, concealing his resentment and still honored by his neighbors. Then, with the resignation of Richard Cromwell, when none could tell what would happen in England, the Assembly elected him governor. Although in his mind it was treason to hold office from any save the King, he consented, reserving the right to surrender his commission in case the monarchy was restored. A few years later Charles II sent him a new commission and for seventeen more years he was to preside over the colony; but as the Mr. Hyde, not Dr. Jekyll; as the villain of the plot, not the hero.

In the meanwhile, the golden epoch of the Virginia yeomanry was beginning to wane. Hundreds of poor Englishmen continued to pour in each year, new land was taken up, the door to advancement continued open; but the struggle was now harder, the rewards not so great. This unfortunate change began with an act of Parliament in 1651 excluding foreign merchants from the carrying trade between England and her colonies, which doubled freight rates and greatly reduced the planter's margin of profit. Loud were the complaints against the "heartless" merchants who now gave less for tobacco and charged more for English manufactured goods.

With the Restoration matters became worse. New acts were passed which practically annihilated the colony's foreign trade, by making England the only market for its tobacco and the only producer of its imports. This policy was designed to solidify and strengthen the empire by binding the colonies more closely to the mother country, but for Virginia it proved disastrous. Holland, which had served as a distributing center for tobacco, was at a stroke cut off from the trade and England for the time being found that she could not fill her place. So the leaf poured into London and Bristol, where it piled up in the warehouses, while the merchants sought vainly to dispose of it. Before one year's crop was sold another would come in to disrupt the market and send prices lower and lower.

The planters, especially the yeomanry who tilled the fields with the labor of their own two hands, were faced with ruin. "Twelve hundred pounds is the medium of men's yearly crops," wrote Secretary Thomas Ludwell in 1667, "and a half penny per pound is certainly the full medium of the price given for it." This made the average income only fifty shillings, which left the poor man, after he had paid his taxes, very little with which to clothe himself and his family. "So much too little," he added, "that I can attribute it to nothing but the mercy of God that he has not fallen into mutiny and confusion."

It is probable that the small planters did not understand fully the operation of the Navigation Acts, but it was as clear as day that when the Dutch had come into their rivers tobacco had been high and manufactured goods cheap; and that after they had been excluded imports were high and tobacco cheap. There were many earnest discussions at the county seats on court days, or in the church yard after Sunday services, or when people congregated for marriages, or dances, or funerals. Why should the planters be sacrificed for the greedy English merchants? Were not the laws in reality an unjust and oppressive tax upon the colony, laid without the consent of the colonists themselves? Should not the Assembly, as the guardians of the people's interests, make a formal protest to the King?

In this matter of the English trade laws Governor Berkeley was in full sympathy with the planters. But he was not the man to consent to a popular protest, for that in his mind would have smacked of treason, would have been following in the footsteps of the House of Commons in the days of Charles I. But he himself set sail for England to plead the cause of the colony at Court and explain the ruinous consequences of the trade laws. "We cannot but resent," he said, "that 40,000 people should be impoverished to enrich little more than forty merchants, who being the whole buyers of our tobacco, give us what they please for it. And after it is here sell as they please, and indeed have 40,000 servants in us at cheaper rates than other men have slaves, for they find them meat and drink and clothes. We furnish ourselves and their seamen with meat and drink, and all our sweat and labor as they order us will hardly procure us coarse clothes to keep us from the extremities of heat and cold."

But Sir William could do nothing. The trade laws were necessary to build up English navigation and manufactures, he was told, and to knit the empire together and make it strong enough to resist attack. The fault lay with the planters themselves. Instead of flooding England with tobacco, which could neither be consumed there nor reexported, let them turn their attention to the production of silk, or pig iron, or glass, or pitch and tar, or wine, all of which were greatly needed by the mother country. Berkeley seems for the moment to have been persuaded, for he promised that in seven years Virginia would be pouring basic commodities into the British market. But in the end his efforts not only proved futile, but cost the colony thousands of pounds sterling and so added to the distress.

Equally unsuccessful was his attempt to put through a seventeenth-century Agricultural Adjustment Act. The situation of the planters was quite similar to that of the cotton and the wheat growers of today, who have so long been troubled with the shrinking of their foreign market and the resulting decline in prices. And the recent expedients to cut down production—the slaughter of hogs, the restrictions on potato growing, the payments to farmers for limiting their acreage of wheat, cotton and other crops—had their forerunner in Berkeley's attempt to secure a tobacco "stint" nearly three centuries ago. If a law could be passed prohibiting tobacco growing for a year, it was thought, the glut in England would clear up and prices approach their old level.

For such a measure to be effective, however, it had to be carried out not only in Virginia, but in Maryland and North Carolina as well. In 1662 planters and merchants combined in a petition to Charles II, to order a cessation of planting for a year, but since a very appreciable part of his revenue was derived from the customs duty on tobacco, he gave an emphatic refusal. Later, as matters went from bad to worse, he so far relented as to authorize the colonies to make some restrictions if they could agree among themselves. Accordingly commissioners from Virginia and Maryland, meeting in 1664, recommended acts forbidding the planting of tobacco in any year until after June 20, but their efforts came to naught when the Maryland Assembly withheld its consent.

Now followed long and discouraging negotiations. At one time Berkeley made a journey to Maryland in the dead of winter to explain and argue and plead. When at last the Marylanders were convinced and agreed to prohibit planting for a year, the North Carolinians delayed following suit until it was too late. At last, when success seemed to have crowned Berkeley's efforts, and all three colonies agreed to a cessation, Lord Baltimore "in absolute and princely terms" refused to sanction it. "This overtook us," wrote Sir William, "like a storm and enforced us like distressed mariners to throw our dear bought commodities into the sea, when we were in sight of our harbor, and with them so drowned not only our present reliefs but all future hopes." This selfish act "raised the grief and anger" of the people "of this colony to such a height as required great care to prevent those disturbances which were like to rise from their eluded hopes."

For Peter Bottom this is a time of tragedy. We find him still working hard on his plantation, assisted now not only by an indentured worker, but his own sturdy son. He has made many new clearings in the forest, for his old fields, exhausted by repeated crops, are covered with a growth of scrub pines. But his little cottage is now but a wing of a larger residence which boasts of a hall, a bedroom or two, and a kitchen. His sliding shutters have given way to casement windows with tiny leaded panes. He owns two beds, several Turkey-worked chairs, a looking glass, two or three chests, a goodly display of pewter and earthen porringers, sugar pots, castors and plates. Nearby is his garden partly devoted to vegetables, partly to phlox and other flowers, partly to currant and gooseberry bushes. Here is his barn, here the hen house, here the milk house, there the crudely built tobacco house where the fragrant leaf is cured, stored and packed for shipment. As he sits under the great trees of his front yard smoking his pipe and thinking of the old days in Essex, he rejoices in the prosperity which his move to the New World has brought him.

A rude awakening is in store.

As usual, when word reaches him late in the autumn that the merchant ships have arrived in the James, he rolls his tobacco casks down to his landing, loads them on his shallop, and shoves off for the voyage down to Bermuda Hundred. Here he finds an English merchantman, and going on board begins to bargain for the sale of his crop. He protests when he is offered a price a full halfpenny below last year, but the captain explains that much of the old crop remains unsold in England and that he must protect himself against loss. Yielding reluctantly, Peter now turns to the purchase of English goods to supply his family and plantation for the ensuing year. He needs clothing, a plow, nails, hinges, gunpowder, shoes, a spinning wheel, thread, a new fire pot, a pestle. But prices of manufactured goods have gone up, and he has to content himself with purchasing only the most urgently needed articles. Perplexed and discouraged he loads his meager purchases on his shallop and heads up stream to his plantation.

The next year he finds conditions worse. Tobacco has sunk to a penny a pound and his crop suffices only for the barest necessities—a few clothes and perhaps the cheapest farm implements without which life on the plantation could not go on. But Peter does not despair; tobacco cannot remain permanently at the bottom, he thinks, and good days will return. Food he has in abundance, for his fields supply him with grain, his cattle with meat, milk, butter and cheese, his garden with vegetables, his orchard with fruit. And though his clothing is wearing out, he can supply his wants to some extent with homespun. So he plants a patch of cotton, buys a few sheep and turns out a coarse yarn upon his spinning wheel which he pays a neighbor who owns a loom to convert into cloth. But the labor is arduous and the results far from satisfactory.

SEEDS OF REBELLION

A decade later, when Bacon had raised the standard of revolt, his followers were derided as ragamuffins and scarecrows. Yet theirs was the raggedness not of hoodlums or idlers but of hardworking men reduced to nakedness by injustice and oppression.

At last came a time when Peter could find no purchaser for his tobacco at any price, for the number of merchant vessels trading in the river was smaller than usual and all available cargo space had been filled with the hogsheads of the wealthy planters. He was forced to return home empty-handed and store his crop over the winter. At all events he could console himself with the thought that with tobacco selling for a farthing a pound nothing was lost by waiting. But when twelve months later he succeeded in finding a purchaser, it was at a price so exceedingly low that it hardly paid him for the trouble of shipping it down the river. By this time his need for money had become so pressing, especially money for farm implements, that he had to have it or curtail production. He could not cut timber with dulled axes or cultivate tobacco with broken hoes. So he was forced to go to one of his wealthy neighbors, a justice of the peace, a burgess, and a favorite of the governor, and give a mortgage on his plantation for a loan of £10. In this way he tided things over for several years, but from now on he was in the power of the ruling group.

In his opposition to the trade laws Sir William was still the warm advocate of the best interests of the colony, still the leader of all the people. Despite his growing peevishness he might have retained his popularity, had he not launched a new policy of repression, with the design of nullifying representative government and making himself the undisputed master of the colony. In this he was actuated not only by his hatred of all things republican, but his growing avarice and appetite for power, his impatience of the least opposition. So he concentrated in his person the legislative, administrative and judicial powers until his warm partisan, Secretary Thomas Ludwell, could declare that he was "the sole author of the most substantial part" of the government, "either for laws or other inferior institutions."

When the burgesses assembled in the little statehouse at Jamestown in March 1661, after the first election of the Restoration period, the governor received them with smiles. Apparently the representatives of the people had suddenly become once more his favorites and the object of his especial favors. One by one he singled them out for offices of profit or honor, making this man a collector of one of the rivers, this one a sheriff, this one a captain in the militia, this one a justice of the peace. To several he seems to have hinted at the possibility of a seat in that august body, the Council of State. It was all very pleasant and the burgesses showed a due sense of gratitude by voting enthusiastically for whatever Sir William proposed. And the governor, to eliminate any possibility of such complaisant men being voted out of office, refused to call for a new election and held them over for another year.

Thus were the people robbed of real representative government. They might consider the burgesses traitors to their cause, but they were helpless so long as Berkeley refused to grant a new election. Year after year the old group of placemen fawned on the governor, and year after year the governor continued his favors and kept them on by prorogation. And if occasionally death or resignation made it necessary to fill individual seats, he only too often secured the election of other favorites by browbeating the voters. "It is true," declared Bacon, "that the people's hopes of redemption did lie in the Assembly, as their . . . sanctuary to fly to, but I would have all men consider how poor people are debarred of their fair election, the great men in many places having the country in their debt and consequently their awe." Berkeley's corrupt Assembly continued fifteen years until the threat of rebellion at last forced him to dissolve it.

As the poor man toiled on his little plantation, now perhaps heavily mortgaged and showing by the dilapidation of barn and fences the ravages of hard times, his soul was filled with bitterness. When the sheriff appeared at his door to levy the colonial, county and parish taxes, he could hardly restrain himself. His little crop did not suffice under the most favorable circumstances to meet his urgent needs. Was it just that a third or more should be taken from him? As for the justices of the peace, many of them men of mean origin and worse ability who had risen to power by fawning upon the governor, what right had they to carry things with so high a hand? Had not some of them obtained their property by bribing the secretary to make out patents for large tracts of land, some by dispossessing poor persons of their farms by unjust suits in the courts, others by helping themselves from the public treasury? Why were they so careful to lock the courthouse door when they met to assess taxes if not for the purpose of concealing their dishonesty and misgovernment?

Moreover, it was entirely wrong that they should have the power to tax at all, since they did not represent the people, but were appointed by the governor. Are we to submit tamely, asked the people, while they reduce us to poverty, draw us into debt, keep us in bondage by their breaches of law and their defiance of justice and carry things as though the colony were fair booty for them to divide among themselves? Is this the liberty promised us and our fathers when we left our homes in England to reclaim this country from the wilderness?

Even religion is made an excuse for oppressing us. We do not object to paying a just portion of our incomes for the minister's salary and the upkeep of the church building, but why should parish dues be apportioned and levied by the vestries? The vestries are self-perpetuating bodies, composed usually of the same group who lord it over us in the county courts, so that we have no control over them whatever. The colonial government is undemocratic, local government is undemocratic, the Church is undemocratic, and the poor man is duped, cheated, oppressed on all sides.

The small farmer's cup of bitterness was filled when he considered the unequal character of taxes, for his share was out of all proportion to his ability to pay. True, the rich were taxed on their indentured workers and slaves, but this by no means ironed out the inequality. Justice demanded that the government be supported by a tax on land, especially upon the great unoccupied tracts held by the governor's favorites. This would not only bring large sums into the treasury, but would force them to relinquish thousands of acres procured through fraud, and thus would throw them open to legitimate settlers.

Attempts to monopolize the natural resources of land, forests, and water power have been common in America. But in no instance have the evils been more glaring, more fraught with danger to the common man than in the colonial period, when the grabbing of vast areas through political "pull" was common. In certain parts of Virginia and Maryland especially this practice threatened at one time to change the whole structure of society, by fostering a kind of mild feudal system in which a few wealthy landlords—the Fairfaxes, the Carters, the Carrolls—lived upon the rentals of a host of small tenants.

Although in Berkeley's day land-grabbing had not assumed such large proportions, it was serious enough to call for a special clause in his instructions of 1662. The King charged him to be diligent in collecting his quit rents from all who took out titles to "such quantities of land which they never intend to or in truth can occupy or cultivate, but thereby keep out others who would plant and manure the same." Yet before the close of Sir William's second administration the possessions of his chief friends and supporters ringed the plantations about and presented a real obstacle to further settlement. Lawrence Smith, William Byrd, Joseph Bridger, John Carter and others held a mortgage, as it were, upon the future of all who wished to utilize the best virgin soil of the frontier. And there were hundreds of poor men, toiling on their barren or worn-out farms, who cast their eyes in bitterness at the great expanses thus closed to them.

As for the taxes, protests would have been less vehement, had the money been wisely expended. But there was evidence that much had been wasted and some stolen. What sense was there in trying to build a city at Jamestown at the public charge? If there were need for a city it would develop of its own accord without help from the treasury. So long as the plantations were located on water deep enough to float ocean-going vessels and the farmers could ship their tobacco directly from their wharves, Virginia would be an entirely rural country and Jamestown no more than a hamlet. So the act of the Assembly providing for the erection of thirty-two houses there, and requiring each county to shoulder the responsibility for one, was not only burdensome but futile. Everyone was a witness to the fact that the whole thing had been a failure and some of the costly houses had remained vacant.

Outwardly there was more reason for taxing the people for the erection in each county of tan-houses and plants for "the better converting wool, flax, hemp" into cloth, and for "instructing poor children in the knowledge of spinning, weaving and other useful occupations." Since the exports of tobacco no longer sufficed to provide clothing and shoes for the colonists, it seemed wise for the Assembly to stimulate local production. When the farmer's cow died, or when he butchered a calf, he could bring the hide to the county tan-house to have it converted into leather for shoes for himself and his family. If he possessed a spinning wheel and made his own yarn, the county weaver would be ready to convert it into cloth.

Unfortunately, this experiment in socialism, certainly one of the earliest in American history, proved a dismal failure. Besides other taxes, complained the people of Charles City county, "great quantities of tobacco have been raised on us for building . . . houses of handicraft and manufactury." Yet absolutely nothing had been accomplished save the enriching of the contractors, "who were largely rewarded for thus defrauding us," since the plants had not even been completed or put into operation. The 11,000 pounds of tobacco assessed on this county to erect the tan-house had been embezzled and the taxpayers "utterly defrauded."

As time wore on and the people suffered one disaster after another, some said that it was not only the King and his governor who frowned on Virginia, but God himself. No one could blame Sir William for the "prodigious hailstorm" which struck the colony in April 1667, when lumps of ice as big as turkey eggs came pelting down, destroying the newly planted crops and killing livestock. It was not his fault that in June it began raining and continued without intermission for forty days, so that the wheat, rye and oats planted after the hailstorm rotted in the ground. But the worst calamity was the hurricane of August 27, of the same year. The wind blowing with great force was accompanied by a torrential rain, and for twenty-four hours the terrified people listened to the roar of the storm and the crash of falling houses. When at last the sun rose the next morning, it revealed a scene of utter desolation—ruined barns and tobacco houses, fences down, the tobacco "torn to pieces" in the fields, trees blown over, rowboats and sloops stranded high on shore, chimneys wrecked. The tempest swept the waters of Chesapeake Bay up the rivers and creeks until it overflowed the banks, exposed many to drowning "who lived not in sight" of the water and forced them to take refuge on the roofs of their houses.

The planters had not fully recovered from this disaster when another, equally distressing, overtook them. In the winter of 1672-1673 an epidemic broke out among the cattle and carried off the poor beasts by thousands. This was a serious matter indeed, for the small planter used his oxen to draw his cart and perhaps his plow, and he was dependent upon his cows for milk, butter, cheese and meat. It was the custom in Virginia to leave the cattle at large, even in winter, to find their food in old fields, marshes and woods, so that no adequate shelter was provided for them. The winter of 1672-1673 chanced to be unusually cold and this increased the mortality. Many a poor planter, in a desperate effort to prevent the loss of cows and calves, gave them all his store of corn and thus brought hunger upon himself. Before relief came with spring, half the cattle in the colony had perished.

TORCHBEARER OF THE REVOLUTION

Though it was the hand of providence which had delivered these blows, it was the negligence of the King which caused the capture of the tobacco fleet by the Dutch in 1667 and the loss of nine more merchantmen in 1673. The people of the colony were loyal to the throne, they had submitted to the restrictions on their commerce, they were paying thousands of pounds in taxes to the English exchequer through the import duty on their tobacco; in return it was the duty of the King to defend them against attack. Yet during both Dutch wars Chesapeake Bay was so poorly protected that twice a few hostile warships had sailed in between Cape Henry and Cape Charles and played havoc with the merchantmen. In May 1667 there were about twenty vessels, loaded down with hogsheads and ready to sail for England, anchored at the mouth of James River. A few miles above was the *Elizabeth*, a frigate of forty-six guns, which was the sole defense of Virginia and Maryland waters. For the moment, however, the *Elizabeth* was no protection at all, for she was so leaky that she could not keep at sea and her masts were in need of repair.

Such was the situation when, on June 4, a Dutch fleet of five warships under Abraham Crimson sailed in past Hampton Roads and entered the mouth of the James. As they passed the tobacco fleet they lulled the skippers into a sense of security by flying the English colors, hailing them in English and singing out the soundings in English. Sailing up to the *Elizabeth*, they suddenly opened with volley after volley. The frigate could make no resistance, for the captain was on shore making merry at a wedding, and although some of the sailors rushed to the guns they were so entirely unprepared that only one was fired before they were forced to surrender. After securing the *Elizabeth*, the Dutch turned on the tobacco fleet, captured them all, burned five or six, and sailed away with the others.

In 1673 the enemy met sterner resistance, for when they entered the bay with nine warships, they found two British frigates waiting for them. These vessels put up such a gallant fight, tacking in amidst the enemy and firing broadside after broadside, that most of the tobacco ships had time to scurry to shelter, either up the James River or under the guns of Fort Nansemond. Unfortunately no less than nine of them ran aground and so fell into the hands of the Dutch. All in all, hundreds of hogsheads of tobacco were lost in these two disasters and new suffering was inflicted upon the languishing and distracted colony.

Amid the widespread poverty Berkeley might have done much to appease the people had he himself set the example of generosity and thrift. Many a great military leader has inspired his men to deeds of bravery by exposing himself to danger, Napoleon at Arcola, Washington at Princeton. Had the governor volunteered to reduce his own salary, or even to refuse the annual gift of £200 from the Assembly in order to reduce by so much the people's taxes, the effect would have been salutary. But Berkeley greedily accepted every penny he could get his hands on, regardless of the universal suffering and even of threatened rebellion. "Though ambition commonly leaves sober old age," he confessed, "covetousness does not." It seemed monstrous to the debt-ridden small planters that Sir William should have an income of £1,200 over and above his perquisites and the returns of his plantation and other properties. Why, £1,200 was the equivalent of from 300,000 to 400,000 pounds of tobacco, or the output of at least two hundred men.

TORCHBEARER OF THE REVOLUTION

The governor's estate at Green Spring with its "manor" containing the great hall and six rooms, with its many outhouses, its orchards of fifteen hundred apple, peach, apricot, quince and other fruit trees; its wide acres devoted not only to tobacco, wheat and Indian corn but to flax, hemp and cotton; its seventy horses; its servants and slaves, was princely according to the simple standards of early Virginia. The extent of the Green Spring property may be surmised from the fact that the great hall was large enough for a meeting of the Assembly in 1677 and that Berkeley housed there at one time no less than two hundred men, including prisoners and guards. For his own use and the use of Lady Berkeley he owned a coach, one of the first in Virginia, to cover the two miles to Jamestown on sunny days when the road was passable. So in the eyes of the people the avaricious old governor was a veritable nabob who lived luxuriously at their expense.

As the third quarter of the century neared its close the murmurs of the poor planters changed into open complaints and even threats. In their minds the King was still their real friend and protector, and would surely redress their wrongs if only they could reach his ear. But this was almost impossible. The proper channel for the sending of petitions to his Majesty was the Assembly, but the corruption and subservience of that body rendered any hope in that quarter futile, while a remonstrance signed by simple farmers with no official status, even though it might reach England, would never find its way to the King in Council.

So, like any other liberty-loving people, the oppressed yeomen turned their thoughts to righting their wrongs with arms in their hands. In every household there were fusils or muskets or halberds for protection against the Indians, for hunting and for service in the militia. If necessary they would seize them and march on Jamestown to force the governor and his minions to do them justice. So loud were the threats, so ominous the widespread anger, that the government was in a continuous state of apprehension. It was a matter of congratulation at Jamestown that the planters did not make common cause with the Dutch when they invaded the Chesapeake in 1673. The people "speak openly that they are in the nature of slaves," declared one observer, "so that the hearts of the greatest part of them are taken away from his Majesty." Thus the most valuable colony was in danger of going over to the Dutch, with whom they desired to resume their former trade.

The announcement in 1674 that the taxes for that year would be even heavier than before was received with a tremendous burst of anger. In New Kent scores of ragged men collected with arms in their hands, swearing they would prevent collection by force. Only a proclamation by the governor warning them that to resist the royal authority was treason, together with the pleading of several prominent men whom they trusted, induced them to disperse to their homes. That this was not the only incident of the kind we know from Berkeley's statement that he had "appeased" two mutinies, "raised by some secret villains who whispered among the people that there was nothing intended by the fifty pounds [levy] but the enriching of some few people." Had they found a leader at this time, a man of ability and daring, it is probable that these disorders would quickly have developed into open rebellion. Two years later, when to poverty, injustice and oppression had been added the horrors of Indian war, and when a popular hero appeared in the person of young Nathaniel Bacon, the people not only rose against the governor and drove him headlong out of Jamestown, but defied the might of England itself.

In all American history there has been no chapter more depressing than the story of Virginia in the fifteen years following the restoration of Charles II. It was an important period, not only for the colony but for the great nation of which it was destined to become a part, for it was then that the character of southern society was taking form. As we look back upon the struggles of that day we realize that the vital issue was not the despotism of a Berkeley, for that was temporary, not the restrictions on the tobacco trade which in a few decades ceased to be so prejudicial to the planters, not the heavy taxes, not the oppressions of corrupt politicians, but whether England's greatest colony was to be democratic or aristocratic, whether the mass of the people—intelligent, self-respecting, prosperous farmers—were to control the government, or whether there was to be a degraded peasantry held under the heel of the mother country and of a powerful local aristocracy.

Long after Sir William Berkeley and Nathaniel Bacon had been laid in their graves the issue between them was fought out in different guises, on new fronts, by new leaders. Now it was the resistance of the colonies to the English attempt to undermine their liberties by taxing them without their own consent; now the struggle to rid the country of slavery and strike down the society based on it; now the battle against giant business combinations allied with corrupt politicians. But at no time was the danger greater or the assaults on the rights of the people more open and dangerous than in Restoration Virginia, when we have some of the earliest concrete examples of

SEEDS OF REBELLION

certain evils which remained to plague the nation in after years—injustices wrought through trade restrictions, the perversion of justice to the injury of the poor and weak, the plundering of the people with the connivance of their representatives, the grabbing of natural resources.

CHAPTER II
THE SQUIRE OF HENRICO
"OUR HOPES OF SAFETY, LIBERTY, OUR ALL"

The Squire of Henrico

IN THE MEANWHILE, IN FAR-OFF ENGLAND, NATHANIEL BACON was growing to manhood, unconscious that events in Virginia were hastening on toward the final tragedy in which he was to play so important a part. If an occasional letter from his cousin reached Friston Hall, it is unlikely that it dwelt at length upon conditions in the colony, or if there were brief references to the trade laws, or to high taxes, or the hurricane they would be written from the standpoint of the colonial aristocrat, not the friend and advocate of the common people. So young Nathaniel, as the heedless days passed in the old manor house, or at college, or as he travelled open-eyed over Europe, or studied in the famous chambers at Gray's Inn, or entered upon the life of the country squire in his native Suffolk, could have known little about the great injustices against the Virginia yeomanry or their effect upon his destiny.

In later life Nathaniel's enemies charged him with a neglect of religion unbecoming the son of a Suffolk squire of Puritan leanings who had given expression to his piety by building a chapel on his estate. Perhaps the youth's skepticism may be blamed upon the old manorial chaplain, whose "jejune" sermons, delivered in quaint little St. Mary's, were boring to the young as well as the old, and who at afternoon prayers repeated "without addition or alteration" the same words he had delivered in the morning. To Nathaniel religion, as taught by this typical example of the stupid, servile country parson, must have seemed lifeless and unconvincing.

In the Middle Ages young men of noble family, regarding education as fit only for monks and secretaries, schooled themselves chiefly in hunting and tilting. But the squire of the time of Charles II realized that his son could not take his proper place as magistrate, political leader and country gentleman without at least a smattering of the classics, mathematics, philosophy and law. If there chanced to be a good grammar school nearby he entered his son there, otherwise he entrusted him to the chaplain or employed a private tutor. At a very early age the youngster with his luggage was loaded into the family coach and driven off to Oxford or Cambridge. For Nathaniel there could be but one choice, since Cambridge was the traditional university of the Bacon family. In May 1660, at the very moment when in Virginia his future antagonist was entering upon his career of despotism, he left Friston to enter St. Catharine's Hall.

Life at Cambridge was novel and exciting for a boy of thirteen acquainted only with the Suffolk countryside. He must have a tutor, usually known by reputation or personally to the family, to act as friend and guide, direct his reading, supervise his conduct, perhaps administer punishment, keep his funds and pay his steward's bill, tuition, library fees, bills from the bedmaker, the tailor, the barber, the laundress. Nathaniel was fortunate in having as his tutor Samuel Brunning, a young man of about twenty-one, who later became rector of All Saints, at Semer, Suffolk. It was important for the new student to secure an attractive chamber, perhaps in the Claypool building, or the New building at five shillings a quarter, perhaps a room overlooking the master's garden. The square cap which had just replaced the puritanical round cap of Cromwell's time, together with the flowing gown gave the youthful student a sense of dignity and importance.

Since it was customary for the oldest son of a wealthy country gentleman to enter college as a fellow-commoner, Nathaniel joined that group as a matter of course. This was unfortunate. The fellow-commoners paid much higher fees than the pensioners and the sizars and were required to present to the college some costly bit of silver, but in return they enjoyed privileges which tended neither to discipline their characters nor improve their minds. They were usually excused from lectures and in their scorn of academic work were kept in countenance by those who registered as noblemen. Many left without taking a degree and others became Bachelors of Arts after a farcical examination.

The society of the university was far from democratic, for the fellow-commoner looked up to the nobleman and down upon the pensioners. As for the sizars, the sons of poor clergymen, small farmers and artisans, who paid small fees and performed menial services, they were regarded as an inferior class. The day had not yet dawned when a student could wait on the table in hall and retain his social standing. Perhaps the haughty fellow-commoner never once reflected that the sizar who made his bed and dined off the leavings of the other students, was getting a better preparation for life than himself, might some day be a leader in science, or theology, or in the government. It seems strange that Bacon, who in after years was to become the champion of the poor and the oppressed, should have received his early training in this atmosphere of snobbery.

But it is not strange that he should have "broken into some extravagances" which caused his father to withdraw him from college after he had been there less than two and a half years. The fellow-commoner had every temptation to get into trouble, for with no work to do, with his pockets full of money and with many idle companions at hand, he might easily become tired of hunting and hawking, boating, or even watching an occasional bear-baiting on Gogmagog Hills, and begin to frequent the local taverns. It was the easier since breaches of discipline by fellow-commoners were either punished lightly or overlooked entirely. It seems clear that Thomas Bacon withdrew his son chiefly because the boy, who was not overfond of his books, was learning little of good from his teachers and much that was harmful from his associates. After all he might profit more from the instruction and example of a learned tutor, and at Friston he would not be subjected to the many temptations of Cambridge.

So Mr. Bacon wrote to John Ray at Cambridge, inviting him to come to Friston Hall to act as Nathaniel's tutor. This young man was destined to become one of the greatest scientists of his day. The son of a blacksmith, he had gone to Cambridge where he advanced rapidly, taking his Bachelor's and Master's degrees, becoming Minor Fellow, Greek lecturer, mathematics lecturer and college steward in turn. In addition to being an "eminent tutor," a Hebrew scholar, a botanist of the first order, he was an excellent preacher and was ordained deacon in 1660. Ray's views were in harmony with the established Church, but he objected to one minor point in the Bartholomew Act of 1662 and his refusal to subscribe cost him his living at Cambridge. It was this which gave Thomas Bacon the hope that he might be persuaded to come to Friston Hall.

Although the unusually large stipend of £40 a year was suggested with no other duties than taking charge of

Nathaniel's work and superseding the old parson at prayers, Ray at first refused because he had "the design of travelling hot in his head." He wanted to tour Europe to make scientific observations of birds, plants, governments, customs, machines, literatures, antiquities, and was determined not to be diverted. But he finally accepted the position for a few months until preparations could be completed for his journey. In October 1662, we find him settled in his quarters at Friston Hall.

"I have been very kindly entertained and civilly treated here," he wrote, "and may have my own terms if I consent to stay." His young charge he found a lad of "very good parts and a quick wit," but "impatient of labor," so that his temper would not admit of long study. However, "I must needs with gratitude acknowledge and commend his kindness, civility and respectful carriage towards me, whom he studies, as much as he can, to please, gratify and oblige."

It would have been strange indeed had not the bright lad of fifteen become attached to the brilliant scientist of thirty-five, who was his instructor and daily companion. And their walks together over the Suffolk countryside, where every object held its world of interest, did more to arouse Nathaniel's intellectual curiosity than all the lore of his neglected books. It was an especial delight to set traps for birds for observation and classification—a bittern, a curlew, a yarwhelp and an unknown fowl "like a duck, with a bill hooked at the top."

Ray had planned to start on his journey in company with two former pupils, Francis Willughby and Philip Skippon, both destined to become distinguished naturalists, and the time was now approaching. Nathaniel, like any boy under similar conditions, wanted to accompany him and eventually gained the consent both of his father and his tutor. A tour of Europe was quite the thing for the sons of wealthy English squires, and this special tour held out most unusual opportunities. To be the daily companion of three men of elevated character and wide intellectual attainments, to hear their comments on foreign customs or ancient buildings or strange inscriptions, on Italian paintings, or German agriculture, or Dutch transportation was in itself a liberal education.

So in April 1663, we find Nathaniel at Gravesend with Willughby and two servants, embarking on his memorable tour. At Dover, Ray and Skippon joined the company. After visiting the castle, the ruins of an old church and the palace, they all set sail for Calais.

Now followed a series of interesting experiences such as fall to the lot of few boys. The great cities of Europe passed before the tourists as in a drama—Ghent, Brussels, Louvain, Antwerp, Rotterdam, Amsterdam, Coblentz, Zurich, Vienna, Venice, Naples, Genoa, Rome. There were visits to cathedrals inspiring in their grandeur and beauty, to ancient castles, to Jesuit colleges, to Jewish quarters, to famous universities, to great libraries, to medicinal baths. They gazed in wonder at the Strassburg clock, with its little figure which "keeps time at every stroke with a scepter," the twelve apostles who followed one another, and the cock which crowed. There were boat trips on the Dutch canals, wagon rides through the woods and fields and villages, horseback journeys over difficult mountain passes.

At Naples Nathaniel and Willughby separated temporarily from the others and proceeded alone to northern Italy. On their way to Rome, where they planned to rejoin Ray and Skippon, young Bacon fell ill of the smallpox and was interned at Bologna. This incident threatened to bring the lad's wanderings to a tragic conclusion, but he was completely recovered by February 10, 1666, when he rejoined his friends at Venice. When the news of his son's illness reached Thomas Bacon, he sent for him to come home, and in May Nathaniel bade his friends goodbye in Genoa and set out for Paris "intending directly for England."

The years spent under Ray's instruction or during these fascinating travels fail to give us any adequate clue to Nathaniel's future career in Virginia. Ray and Willughby were primarily scientists, not revolutionists or political theorists, and the conversations along the road or in the taverns could hardly have emphasized such topics as representative government or the rights of the people. If mention was ever made of Virginia, it was probably in reference to the strange animals or interesting plants of that distant land, not to the injustice of the trade laws, Berkeley's tyranny or the sufferings of the small planters.

Back at Friston, when the greetings and the recital of his adventures were over, Nathaniel's thoughts turned to the completion of his course at Cambridge. As a young man of nineteen, and too mature for the "extravagances" which had caused his withdrawal, he set out once more to resume his residence at St. Catharine's Hall. Two years later he graduated with the Master of Arts degree. At first sight it would seem strange that he should have been admitted to an advanced degree at the age of twenty-one after less than four years of residence at Cambridge. But the requirements at the time were not rigid and the testimonials of Ray that he had led a scholarly and studious life in his absence would certainly have been accepted.

Having now completed the *grand tour* and secured a university degree, the next step for young Bacon was a course of study in one of the Inns of court. Every country squire was supposed to have a smattering of law so that he could make a pretense of legal learning when he took his seat in the local court. And for Nathaniel the selection of Gray's Inn was just as inevitable as had been the choice of Cambridge. There have been forty-eight members of the Bacon family at Gray's Inn, and young Nathaniel, when he took up residence there, was reminded at every turn of his great kinsman, Lord Francis Bacon. Here were the gardens which he laid out with such loving care and along whose walks he used to stroll arm in arm with Sir Walter Raleigh discussing law, politics and philosophy; here in the library was a collection of his books; here was his portrait hanging in the hall; here were his chambers.

Thomas Bacon entered his son at the Inn on November 22, 1664, when Nathaniel was in Italy, apparently to make sure that there would be a place for him when he had completed his travels and received his degree from Cambridge. Since the author of *Strange Newse from Virginia* states that he studied long in the Inns of court, we may conclude that he was in residence for at least a year or two after 1668.

Even for one who had an aversion to hard study the life at Gray's Inn was a valuable experience. The attendance upon readings, the visits to the law courts, the association with distinguished men, the discussions with other students were broadening and stimulating. Nathaniel probably arrived too late to join the "rebellion" of barristers and students against the benchers in 1667, but his life in the Inn had its full share of interest, with the Christmas revels, the noisy meals in the hall, the strolls in the garden or the nearby fields. Nor could he fail to be inspired by the dignity and beauty of the chapel, its

THE SQUIRE OF HENRICO

windows decorated with figures and armorial bearings; the hall, whose ceiling was reminiscent of Westminster Hall and whose screen was the gift of Queen Elizabeth; the library with its ponderous volumes chained to the shelves.

When Nathaniel finally returned to Friston Hall after years of travel and study, he was a well educated, interesting and accomplished young man. That he should remain there, marry, and eventually succeed to his father's estate and to the life of a wealthy English squire was taken for granted. If he knew anything of what was going on in Virginia—the impoverishing of the small planters by the trade laws, the despotism of Berkeley, the hurricane, the capture of the tobacco fleet by the Dutch—he regarded it with mild interest, ignorant of the vital part it was to play in his own life. Certainly nothing could have seemed more improbable than his migration to the colony.

In fact his thoughts at this time seem to have been concentrated on winning the love of Elizabeth Duke, daughter of Sir Edward Duke of Benhall. Nathaniel's slender figure, his interesting pensive air, his tendency to silences which he could break with fascinating stories of his travels, must have made him very attractive to women. He is described as a man "adorned with many elaborate qualifications," who "usually spoke as much sense in a few words" as any man in England.

At all events, Elizabeth readily yielded her heart. Unfortunately, although nothing would have been more appropriate than an alliance between the two old Suffolk families of Bacon and Duke, when Nathaniel asked Sir Edward for her hand he met with a severe rebuff.

We do not know why Sir Edward was so bitterly opposed to this match. But he closeted himself with his daughter again and again, arguing, pleading and threatening in an effort to make her put Nathaniel out of her mind. When this proved fruitless he tried the threat of disinheritance. It was in April 1670 that he called Elizabeth into his presence and explained the part of his newly drawn will which related to herself. In effect he said:

I have arranged for a legacy of £2,000 to be paid you on the day of your marriage, if you have the consent of your mother, your brother John and my other executors, with the proviso, however, that they must not sanction your marriage with Nathaniel Bacon. If you remain single you are to have £80 a year for life. Also, I once more positively forbid you to marry young Bacon and I repeat that if you disobey me you shall never have a groat from me.

Two thousand pounds was quite a fortune in those days, but Elizabeth did not hesitate to sacrifice it for the man she loved. In May 1670, a few weeks after this last interview with her father, she ran away and married Nathaniel.

When Sir Edward heard that his daughter had defied him, he was so deeply angered that he never again spoke to her or permitted her to come into his presence, steadfastly turning a deaf ear to her pleas for forgiveness. Even on his deathbed he was unrelenting. He charged his son to give her nothing unless she fell into desperate need and then only enough to keep her from starving, for he was resolved to make an example of her for her disobedience. Sir Edward died in January 1671, eight months after Elizabeth's wedding, leaving the major part of his lands, cattle, jewels, plate and other property to his son John.

Years later, when Elizabeth went to law to recover part of her forfeited legacy, a stern, unromantic Lord

Chancellor reproached her for her "presumptuous disobedience." Her father was quite right in cutting her off, he said, for she was forbidden to marry only one man by name, but nothing in the whole fair Garden of Eden would serve her but this forbidden fruit.

Shortly after Sir Edward's death his son, Sir John Duke, had a conference with Nathaniel and Thomas Bacon concerning his sister's maintenance. It was agreed that Nathaniel should settle lands to the value of £60 a year upon her and that Thomas Bacon was to turn over to the young couple lands and tenements worth £40 a year for the term of Nathaniel's life, together with £500 in cash. On his part Sir John gave them £800 in return for a full renunciation of all claims upon the forfeited legacy. With this settlement, which seemed to assure them of an income quite sufficient for their needs, the young Suffolk squire and his bride were well satisfied. Life seemed to stretch out before them happy and uneventful, until with the death of his father, Nathaniel should come into possession of the large estates centering around Friston Hall.

But young Bacon was extravagant and improvident and "could not contain himself within bounds" despite the very "genteel competency" now at his command. It was his carelessness and ignorance in financial matters which involved him in very serious difficulties and caused his father grave misgivings for his future.

A certain William Bokenham and one Peter Phesant, two seventeenth-century sharpers, used him as a catspaw in a scheme to defraud a guileless youth, Robert Jason, out of a part of his inheritance. Bacon sold to Jason for £4,000 certain fields and bullock closes, from property conveyed to him by his brother-in-law, and Jason was to pay when he came into his inheritance upon the death of his father. But when Bokenham got hold of the estate, leaving young Jason empty-handed, Bacon became sensible that an injustice had been done and agreed to cancel the whole arrangement, or if Jason so desired to accept a cash payment of £1,250. But Jason had got himself so involved with Bokenham and Phesant that he could not clear the title of the property, and both he and Bacon came off with nothing more tangible than a long and tedious lawsuit.

At this juncture Thomas Bacon decided that it might be wise for his son to seek his fortune in another land. There he would be upon his own responsibility, could not turn to his father for financial aid in every emergency, and would have to carve out a future for himself. The fact that his cousin, the elder Nathaniel, lived in the colony and had won wealth and high position there must have weighed heavily in the decision of the younger to make Virginia his future home. He could be of great assistance to the young couple in telling them what clothing, utensils, furniture, implements to bring with them, where to purchase a plantation on advantageous terms, in giving instructions in the culture of tobacco, and in advising them as to the best way of escaping the dread Virginia sickness, perhaps even in using his influence to procure for his cousin some office in the government. So Nathaniel's father made him a gift of £1,800 with which to start life in the New World, secured passage for him and his family on a tobacco ship, and in the early summer of 1674 bade them a fond farewell.

King's Creek, the plantation of the elder Nathaniel, must have seemed a strange and interesting place to our young adventurers, with its store on the water's edge where hogsheads of tobacco were waiting shipment for England, the residence not unlike the cottages of Bury

THE SQUIRE OF HENRICO

St. Edmunds where its owner had been baptized fifty-four years before, the garden, the orchard, the tobacco fields, the surrounding woods, the indentured workers, the black slaves some of them conversing in their native tongues, others speaking broken English. But the "large box full of holes" attached to the side of the house where a bevy of martins had built their nests added an English touch to this typically Virginia scene. Although Colonel Bacon was a man of wealth his residence was unpretentious. The house was of brick, one and a half stories in height, with sharply rising roof pierced with dormers, the exterior chimneys at the gable-ends. Within was the new hall, the old hall, Mrs. Bacon's chamber, and three upper chambers, besides the kitchen, the dairy and the storeroom which, as in all Virginia estates, were detached from the main residence. The "outer" room mentioned in Colonel Bacon's inventory was probably added at a later date.

Yet there was ample room to make the travellers comfortable, and the trundle beds, the canvas mattresses stuffed with feathers, the Holland sheets, the worsted rugs, the Turkey-worked chairs, the pewter basins and ewers, the table, the silver dishes, the great fireplace, were luxurious indeed after the hardships of the ocean voyage.

When the two Nathaniels had greeted each other there must have been many inquiries by the older man concerning friends and relations in England and the changes which had taken place in the years since his departure. The two Elizabeths, who had never seen each other before, could find topics of mutual interest in domestic and social affairs—the management of negro servants, the preparation of the distinctive Virginia dishes, the proper dress for the hot summer, the remoteness of the neighbors, the inconvenience of attending church or going to a wedding or a dance by boat or on horseback through the woods.

The younger Nathaniel no doubt heard from his cousin much that was discouraging about conditions in the colony, how the trade laws had driven down the price of tobacco and increased freight rates and the cost of imported goods.

But he had staked his all on Virginia, had brought his family across the Atlantic, and it was now too late to draw back. So it was necessary to look around for a favorable location where a plantation could be purchased for a reasonable sum, and where the soil had not been exhausted by many successive crops. His cousin was well qualified to advise him. It might be wise to settle far back in the country where Elizabeth would not be so apt to fall a victim to the Virginia sickness, where fresh land was abundant but where water transportation was available for shipping out the tobacco hogsheads and receiving European goods. Such a place was Henrico, and Colonel Bacon had a neighbor, Colonel Thomas Ballard, who owned several pieces of property in that county.

There must have been prolonged negotiations with Colonel Ballard. Nathaniel would want to know the exact location of the properties, how much of the land was "fresh" or uncleared for cultivation, what pasturage there was for cattle, what were the facilities for shipping; Elizabeth would be interested in the residence, the number of rooms, the furniture, the linen, the garden, the orchard.

The main plantation which Ballard offered for sale was on the James River about forty miles above Jamestown and twenty miles below the falls. It had formerly been called Longfield, but more recently was named Curles

THE SQUIRE OF HENRICO

Neck because it was located on the famous curles of the river. Although the patent for this land had been granted in 1638, Ballard succeeded in convincing Nathaniel that the soil was still fertile, and on August 28, 1674, the sale was consummated. Bacon bought the land, buildings, cattle and servants for £500, agreeing to pay £200 upon the signing of the deed, £100 in 1675 and the remaining £200 in 1676. Included in the sale was probably the quarters, or plantation to be supervised by an overseer, at the falls of the James which Bacon owned at the time of his death.

As the newcomers sailed up the James to take possession of their home, they must have looked out in wonder at the broad expanse of the river, with its many tributaries, the great forests of oak, hickory, walnut, elm and chestnut, the plantation clearings, the tobacco fields, an occasional farmhouse or possibly a church or two. Jamestown, the little capital of the colony, was but a cluster of houses embedded in the trees and surrounded by marshes and cultivated fields. From the river the tower of the church showed plainly, near it the fort and a row of buildings, one of which was the State House. There was much tacking and turning as the vessel moved on into the crooked upper reaches of the river past Ward's Creek, Merchants Hope, Bermuda Hundred, Turkey Island to Curles Neck.

As Elizabeth stepped ashore she saw on the heights above her a house which must have been in the style of the typical Virginia plantation cottage, a one and a half story structure, forty-five feet by twenty, with brick chimneys at each end, a plain front door flanked by casement windows, the roof covered with cypress shingles. Inside one found the hall or living room with massive fireplace and simple but charming mantel and panelling, a bedroom and in the loft two chambers. Nearby were smaller buildings for kitchen, dairy and servants' quarters, the vegetable garden, the orchard and perhaps a simple bed of flowers.

To Elizabeth such a house would seem crude indeed compared with her father's residence with its great hall and its thirty-two fireplaces; the surrounding country a wilderness compared with the Suffolk countryside. Yet the situation was one of beauty, even grandeur. From the residence, which stood on a fifty- or sixty-foot bluff, one looked directly down upon the James, whose clear waters passed by in a majestic sweep. On the opposite bank was low, marshy ground covered with trees, and far away to the left the fields and woods of Bermuda Hundred tinted deep blue by the haze over the river. The farm hugged the left bank for a mile or two, descending gradually until it was lost in the wooded marshes still known today as Longfields.

This part of Henrico was not on the frontier. Six decades had passed since Sir Thomas Dale had built the picturesque little town of Henricopolis several miles up the river from Curles and in more recent years settlements had been made twenty-five or thirty miles further up the river above the falls. On all sides of the Bacons were plantations whose proprietors welcomed them as interesting and valuable additions to the neighborhood. On the same "neck of land" was Bremo, owned by Richard Cocke, while to the northeast lived Thomas Cocke, at Malvern Hill. Turkey Island plantation, on Turkey Island Creek, was the home of James Crews, who was to become one of Bacon's most devoted friends.

Around the bend of the river to the west was Varina, the hamlet which served as the county seat of Henrico. Here was the courthouse, a little frame structure set up on blocks of wood in place of a foundation, where the justices held their sessions. Nearby were the jail, the ducking stool, the parsonage and the tavern. On court days the village took on an animated appearance, for people came from miles up and down the river to listen to the cases, to trade horses, to make purchases at the store and only too often to get drunk. Elizabeth must have been especially interested in the Rolfe house nearby, where John Rolfe is said to have brought his bride, the Indian princess Pocahontas, to settle on land granted him by her father, Powhatan.

The neighborhood was not without its amusements. Occasionally there was a horse race at the courthouse or at Colonel Eppes' store, or at Malvern Hill. Muster day, when the trained bands assembled to drill and practise arms, drew hundreds of interested spectators. Since the plantations were stretched out along the James which afforded the chief, almost the only, means of transportation, on court days, or muster days, or on Sundays a miniature fleet of rowboats and sloops were tied up at the wharves at Varina or at the church. Attendance at divine services afforded a welcome relief from the monotony of plantation life, for neighbors and friends came early and lingered after the sermon to gossip and talk over politics and crops. But they listened attentively to the sermons of the Reverend John Ball, and were so shocked when a certain Samuel Mathews declared him "fitter to make a hangman than a minister," that they hauled him into court on a charge of libel.

At Bacon's quarters on the site of Richmond conditions were different. Here was the real frontier, and the overseer would have to clear away trees and underbrush to prepare for the tobacco crop and build fences to confine the cattle, erect houses for the indentured workers and slaves, a barn, a tobacco house and a wharf for the sloop. Nearby was the deep forest, where one could hear the howling of wolves at night and where deer and other large game were to be found in abundance. But the workmen at the quarters were not without neighbors. Across the river was the plantation and trading post of William Byrd, where one might see groups of Indians—Occaneechees from the Roanoke River or even Cherokees and Tuscaroras from the far southwest—bartering off their beaver furs and deer skins for the knives, blankets and firearms of the white men. Bacon himself thought of venturing upon this lucrative trade and actually erected a storehouse, but he was diverted from the design, possibly because the governor refused him a license. Sir William himself made a large profit from furs and skins and was averse to new competition. Bacon afterwards stated that he gave up his plan because he saw the folly of supplying the Indians with firearms.

Nathaniel could not have been in Henrico a week without hearing complaints of the low price of tobacco. In conversations with his new friends, at the courthouse or after church services, the important topic was the poverty of the planters, the impossibility of disposing of the crops at a profit, the scarcity and high prices of imported goods, the oppressions by the small group of wealthy men. It did not matter that the rich themselves were sufferers and had complained of the trade laws to the British government. The poor man saw only that they seemed to be prospering, that they usually found purchasers for their crops, that they were extending their land holdings, and that they were threatening to foreclose on his little plantation.

Bacon was deeply impressed by the sufferings of the poor planters and the injustice to which they were sub-

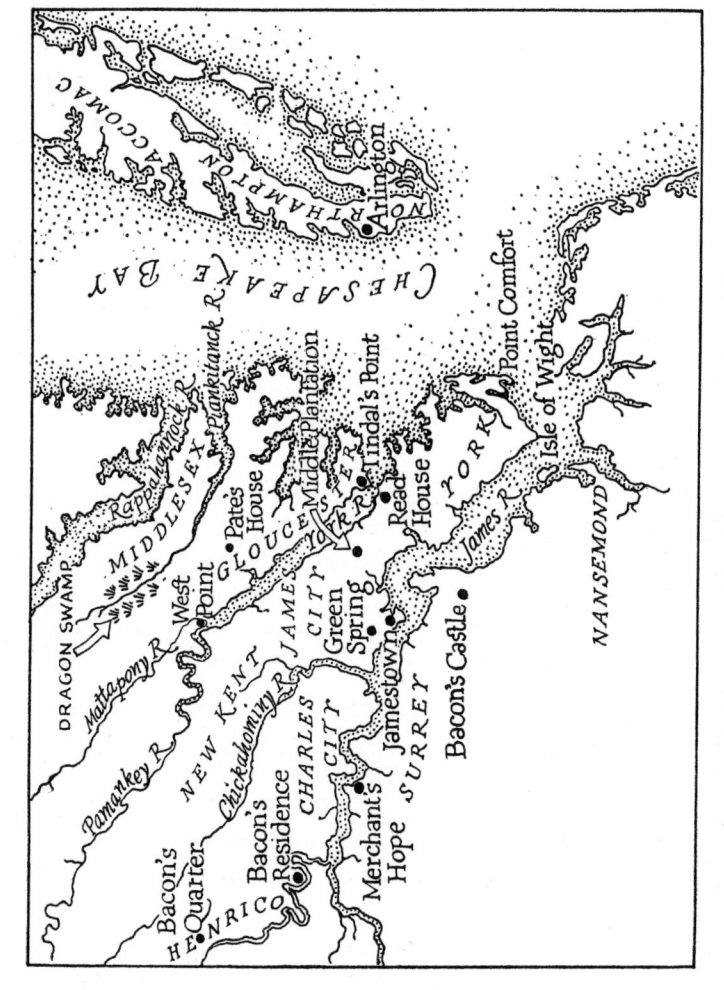

MAP OF VIRGINIA DURING THE TIME OF BACON'S REBELLION

jected. Any unprejudiced man, he said, can see for himself how the rich have oppressed the common people by levying exorbitant taxes, depriving them of their rights and denying them redress in the courts. The poor man's bondage is perpetual, for once he has got into debt it is not possible for him to extricate himself through hard work and economy. Is it right that the men at the helm should run things as though the colony were their booty to be divided up among themselves? As for redress, what hope is there in appealing to the government which is made up of the very persons who should be made to disgorge. It is true that the people's hopes did lie in the Assembly as their sanctuary to which they could fly, but this too has failed them. Consider how the poor people have been intimidated at the polls, how few men there are of learning, ability and courage, nay honesty, to stand up in their behalf; consider how freedom of speech has been suppressed and those who complain have been frowned down and threatened.

Bacon could see at a glance that his material welfare depended upon linking his fortunes with those of the ruling party. He was a man of education and good family, his cousin was in a post of great responsibility and in high favor with Sir William and he could look forward to rapid preferment as sheriff or collector or perhaps in time as councillor of state. But his sense of justice, his love of liberty, his sympathy for the oppressed gave him no stomach for this rôle. The poor men of the colony, many of them his neighbors, had come to Virginia under the promise that they would sacrifice none of the liberties and privileges of Englishmen, and they expected to enjoy on the banks of the James the same right of jury trial, habeas corpus, representative government, protection of property, freedom of speech, as had been theirs in England.

Was it just that England, now that they had staked their all in this new country, should impoverish them by discriminating trade laws? Was it right that the King's governor should oppress them, rob them of real representative government, turn their courts into a farce and overwhelm them with unequal taxes?

In the meanwhile there were other things to demand Nathaniel's attention and keep him busy. He had to acquaint himself with all the details of tobacco cultivation which he had now taken up as his vocation and upon which his future prosperity depended. His neighbors could give him advice and instruction, but he would have to lean heavily upon his overseers. He must know how to prepare the soil, how to distinguish between Orinoco and Sweetscented, how to lay out his bed, transfer the tender plants to the fields, protect them from the tobacco fly, keep the patches free of weeds, remove the suckers, cut off the top, pick off the worms. When the leaf began to ripen he must know how to gather in his crop and carry it to his tobacco houses to hang the leaves on pegs to cure, how to remove the stems and assort the leaves according to grade and variety, how to build hogsheads of the size prescribed by law and pack the tobacco in them, how to secure the best prices from the merchants, roll his hogsheads to the wharf, load them on his sloop, sail down the river to the waiting merchant vessels and with the aid of the sailors hoist the heavy casks on board. There must have been frequent trips up the crooked James to supervise the conduct of affairs at the quarters, while the calls upon his time because of sickness among his servants and slaves or because the barn or tobacco house or fences needed mending or the calves had to be branded were incessant.

THE SQUIRE OF HENRICO

In the midst of these activities Bacon received information that he had been appointed a member of the Council of State. This was a great honor indeed. The Council was composed of the wealthiest and most influential men in the colony, who through long residence, business ability, political acumen or other qualities of leadership had worked their way to the top. They served as a Cabinet to the governor, advising him on all administrative matters; they were the upper House of Assembly; and constituted the supreme court to which all important legal decisions were referred. Upon the councillors the governor had always heaped favors as members of his immediate political household, but in return he expected obedience and support. In short the Council corresponded roughly to the House of Lords and the councillors were in a very real sense untitled noblemen.

At first sight it is surprising that Berkeley should have selected for such a position a young man of twenty-eight who had been in Virginia about one year, who did not possess riches, and whose abilities had not been put to the test. It has been assumed by historians that Nathaniel Bacon, senior, used his influence with the governor to secure the appointment. It is far more probable that the seat came as a bribe. Berkeley was obviously disquieted at Bacon's sympathy with the poorer class, his resentment at the oppressions of the "great men" and his tendency to set himself up as a leader in the popular cause. It would be good policy to transform him into his own partisan and henchman.

It was on March 3, 1675, at a meeting of the General Court that the announcement was made that Mr. Nathaniel Bacon, together with several others, "are made choice of to be of the Council." Bacon himself was not present at the time, but a messenger seems to have been sent off to Curles to notify him, for three days later he took his seat.

Bacon found Jamestown a picturesque, straggling village. Located upon a peninsula in the James River shaped somewhat like an Indian moccasin, and connected with the north bank by a narrow isthmus, it was supposed in the days of Captain John Smith and Sir Thomas Dale to be impregnable to attack by the Indians. But the ground was low and marshy, mosquitoes abounded and before the advent of Peruvian bark there had been much sickness.

One riding into town passed over the isthmus and continued down the old "great road" past Pitch and Tar Swamp into Back Street. After passing a farmhouse or two one came directly upon the State House block to the right of the road, the most imposing group of buildings in Virginia. Stretching out from north to south they comprised five separate structures, the State House, Philip Ludwell's three houses and the so-called country house, supposed to have been Berkeley's residence when he was in town, all joined together as though they were on a street of a crowded English city rather than on an open green in a colonial village. Nor did the architecture differ greatly from that of many an English town, for Bacon must have noted the familiar brick façades pierced by casement windows, their tiny green diamond panes glistening in the sun, the square Gothic porches or entries, the steep roofs covered with tiles, the towering chimney stacks. Directly beyond, on the river bank was the brick fort shaped like a carpenter's square, but dilapidated and ill equipped.

On the north side of Back Street, almost in line with the State House block, was the residence of Richard Lawrence, an Oxford graduate and favorably known "for wit, learning, and sobriety." Although Lawrence was a close neighbor of Sir William, he bore him no good will, for some years before the governor is said to have rendered an unjust decision to oblige "a corrupt favorite" depriving him of a considerable estate. In after times, Lawrence was to be one of Bacon's staunchest friends. Proceeding down Back Street one came to the brick church, the pride of Jamestown. To Bacon, however, it must have seemed a typical village church, its square tower, rising above the tree tops, pierced with slit-like openings, the Gothic windows, the brick mullions, the buttresses, the leaded casements reminiscent of his own St. Mary's at Friston or the little church at Benhall Lodge.

Further on one came to the main part of the village directly east of the church. Here were the ruins of three houses which had burned five years previously, one of which had long served as Berkeley's residence. Here was the Jonathan Newell house, the Walter Chiles house, the Phipps house, the Nicholas Meriwether house, the Knowles house, the William Sherwood house, the Theopholis Hone house and probably the Thomas Swann house.

Recent excavations at Jamestown have disclosed foundations, bits of casements, quarrels of glass, fragments of tiles and plaster, hinges, locks, latches, so that it is now possible to reconstruct the typical residence of the town with every assurance of accuracy. Apparently it differed little from the usual Virginia country residence. It was a one and a half story cottage built of brick, with great exterior chimneys at either end rising in successive stages from a broad base to one or at most two stacks, the windows unevenly spaced on either side of the front door, the roof pierced by dormers and covered by tiles or wooden shingles. Many of the houses were used as ordinaries or taverns when the Assembly or the General Court was in session, where the burgesses, councillors and litigants could secure lodging and food at "extraordinary rates." Just north of the town was Pitch and Tar Swamp and to the east Orchard Run over which Back Street was carried on a bridge. Although the village with its simple cottages, its barns, its surrounding groves, tobacco fields and swamps may have seemed primitive to Bacon, it was at the period of its greatest prosperity, when its people were proud of the twelve new brick houses, the State House and the church.

The oath as a councillor was always administered by the governor in the Council chamber of the State House. This building, erected in 1666, was seventy-seven feet by twenty, two stories high, its roof dominated by two rear chimney stacks. One stepped through the porch into a large apartment used as a waiting room by persons to be summoned before the court, while to the left was the Council chamber or courtroom. A winding staircase in a rear projection led to the Long Room, or burgesses' hall, probably extending the whole length of the building, and a little room over the porch occupied at this time by the secretary of the colony. In the Council chamber there was a platform raised above the main level of the floor and probably separated from it by a railing, where each councillor and justice had his appointed seat.

As Bacon advanced to take the oath from the governor he saw before him a man of sixty-nine, with dark piercing eyes, rounded cheeks, small mouth which gave a false impression of weakness, double chin and large nose. There was in his face the look of one who was accustomed to command, but none would suspect at first glance the smouldering fires of malice that could render him capable of the extremes of hatred, cruelty and revenge.

As he handed out the Bible, Bacon swore to be a true and faithful servant of the King, to be of assistance to the governor, to declare his mind freely according to his heart and conscience, to keep secret the confidential concerns of the Council, and to defend the royal domains against foreign encroachment. Having concluded, he took his seat in the Council beside Sir Henry Chicheley, Colonel Thomas Swann, Colonel Joseph Bridger, Henry Corbin, his cousin Nathaniel Bacon, senior, and other "great men" of the colony.

It is obvious that Bacon was not won over to the governor by his elevation to the Council. He realized that he had nothing to gain by bearding the old man or calling to his attention the distress of the people when the little group sat around the Council table or took their accustomed seats as members of the General Court. Sir William was not open to reason and was quick to resent any opposition, or restraint on his arbitrary rulings. So Bacon contented himself for the present with absenting himself as much as possible. He was not present at any of the sessions of the Court in June 1675. On the one day he attended during the September meeting what he saw and heard must have confirmed his opinion of Berkeley's overbearing conduct.

There resided in Virginia at this time a certain Giles Bland, who had come over to settle an estate for his father and who had received an appointment as collector of customs. Perhaps he had not been in the colony long enough to realize the folly of opposing the governor, perhaps his disposition would not permit him to submit tamely to injustice. At all events he penned a letter to Sir William which sent him into a towering rage. Summoning Bland before the General Court, he read the letter aloud, at the same time declaring the accusations "false, scandalous and mutinous." Arising from his seat and stepping down from the platform, the old man turned to the councillors and demanded that they take immediate action to vindicate him and give satisfaction. Thereupon they voted unanimously to commit Bland to custody and to suspend him from his collector's office. It is highly probable that the accusations against Berkeley were true, and that every man in the room knew they were true; it is also probable that some of those present admired Bland for his directness and his boldness. But one of them had a private quarrel of his own with Bland, others were involved equally with the governor and realized that to disobey him would bring upon them his burning wrath. This scene seems to have cured Bacon of attending the General Court for several months, for he was absent at all the sessions until March 20, 1676, when he resumed his seat for a day and a half only.

Back in Henrico he found the air full of complaints and listened with sympathy all the greater because of what he had witnessed at Jamestown. Although he himself was exempt from taxation as a member of the Council, he pitied the hard condition of many of his neighbors. He saw them laboring from early till late, preparing the soil with their hoes, for few had plows, laying out their little crops, tending them with their own hands or perhaps with the aid of a son or two, building their fences and barns, caring for their cows and pigs. He saw their wives drudging in the garden, or preparing food, or milking the cows, or spinning, or trying to teach the children from the worn-out hornbook. It seemed hard indeed when they had so little that the sheriff should take so large a part of their tobacco crop.

In this crisis the colony needed a governor whom they could trust and respect. Had Berkeley not forfeited his former popularity by his corrupt rule, his contempt for private rights, his improper use of the patronage, his irritability, his singling out of individuals for oppression, he might have led the colony through all its troubles until the advent of better times. Strangely enough, Berkeley prided himself on his ability as a ruler. When he finally resigned the government into the hands of his successor, Colonel Herbert Jeffreys, he was frank enough to write: "I will confess to you that I believe that the inhabitants of this colony will quickly find a difference between your management and mine." Moreover, he had some good qualities. He was a brave and able soldier, he was loyal to his King, he was a fond husband, he was true to his friends. But he was bigoted, narrow in mind and in heart, vindictive, avaricious, fond of power.

Although he lived in Virginia for over thirty-four years, he was never a Virginian. He had no understanding of the forces which gripped the Englishmen who came to the colony to make them self-reliant and liberty-loving—the life upon the plantation, isolation, the vast distance from the mother country. And since he had not lived in England since 1642, England for him remained as it had been in 1642. Therefore the Virginia which he envisaged and tried to shape was based on the England not of Charles II but of Charles I. The Cavalier Parliament might be disobedient to the King and stint him on supplies, but his own Long Assembly must be a "rubber stamp," the people must do homage to him as the representative of his holy Majesty. In short he was out of step with the times, oblivious of the great forces for change, trying to reshape society to fit an outgrown ideal. He would have been crushed had he known that his idol, the "sacred" Charles II considered him just an "old fool."

CHAPTER III
THE INDIAN TERROR

"THAT BLOOD THE HEATHEN DREW INTO A FLOOD"

The Indian Terror

BEFORE BACON CAME TO VIRGINIA IT IS IMPROBABLE THAT he had ever seen an Indian. But like everyone else in England he had heard stories of the Indian character and customs and perhaps had read descriptions in books of travel. He knew, no doubt, that they were warlike, brave and cruel; that they lived by hunting, fishing and primitive agriculture; that they built houses of boughs and bark and protected them by palisades; that their weapons were made of stone and their boats hollowed out of tree trunks. But for the student at Gray's Inn or the young Suffolk squire these accounts had merely an academic interest. Not until he had come to Virginia and established himself on the frontier did he know the Indians at first hand and learn something of their history.

Sixty-seven years had elapsed since the Indians launched their first attack on the English, and there were no eyewitnesses left to describe that memorable scene. But accounts must have been handed down to sons and grandsons of the terror of the men working in the fields outside the little fort at Jamestown when a warwhoop sounded from the surrounding woods, followed by a shower of arrows. They dropped their hoes and fled to the fort, several hundred savages at their heels. For a moment it seemed that the enemy might storm the palisades, for they came up to the gates, riddled the tents within and wounded many of the English, including four of the councillors. Nor could they be driven off until the

TORCHBEARER OF THE REVOLUTION

guns of Captain Newport's ships were brought to bear on them, when they retired without panic, taking with them their dead and wounded.

Thus began the long struggle for the possession of the continent. In Virginia the contest was marked by terrible massacres, bloody raids, by pillaging, burnings and the torturing of captives, by ruthless wars of revenge and the practical extermination of whole tribes. No colony suffered more from the savages than Virginia, not even Massachusetts or New York.

The fact that most of the Virginia tribes were confederated under the leadership of Powhatan made the situation difficult for the English. At any moment this powerful chief might summon his warriors from the Potomac to the Appomattox to the number of 2,500 to hurl them upon the plantations. Nothing saved the colony in its infancy but the white man's superior arms, for the bows and arrows of the Indians made little impression on his helmets and breastplates, while their own naked bodies had no adequate protection against ball and shot. As it was, the Indians, by cutting off small parties, surprising outlying posts and restricting the area of settlement, inflicted great damage and hindered the development of the colony.

So there was great rejoicing when a romantic marriage brought peace between the two races. In the spring of 1613 the English captured Powhatan's daughter, Pocahontas, and held her at Jamestown as a hostage for her father's good behavior. Here her gentle nature, her intelligence and her dignified bearing won the love of Captain John Rolfe, who sought permission to marry her. Governor Dale and Powhatan both gave their assent, and the ceremony was performed in the quaint little wooden church at Jamestown. This wedding brought

THE INDIAN TERROR

about a treaty of peace and a league of friendship which was faithfully observed so long as Powhatan lived. It played an important part in the expansion of the colony. "The great blessings of God have followed this peace," said Rolfe, "and it, next to Him, has bred our plenty—every man sitting under his own fig tree in safety, gathering and reaping the fruits of their labor with much joy and comfort."

But Pocahontas went to England where she died and soon after her father followed her to the grave. His successor, the crafty Opechancanough, realizing that the English were gradually taking possession of the country, determined to wipe them out with one lightning blow. Without declaring war and with great stealth, he gathered his warriors and at the appointed hour fell upon the unsuspecting English. In some places the savages sat down to breakfast with their victims and then suddenly turned on them to butcher men, women and children before they could seize their weapons. No less than 357 persons were slaughtered, including six members of the Council, and only a timely warning by an Indian boy saved Jamestown and the colony.

The war which followed this treacherous deed was venomous. The English found it difficult to bring the Indians to battle, for the natives fled into the forest at the first approach of any formidable expedition. So they hit upon the plan of going out when the maize was just beginning to ripen to cut down the enemy's crop and threaten them with starvation. On one occasion, when Governor Wyatt led an expedition of sixty fighting men against the Pamunkeys, the savages attacked him with eight hundred warriors, determined to save their food supply. But the little band of whites, encased in medieval armor and armed with fusils, not only beat them off but destroyed maize enough "to have sustained four thousand men for a twelve-month." Year after year this deadly war continued and we find the Council so late as 1629 preparing an expedition as usual "to go against the Indians and utterly destroy them."

Even after peace was concluded and the natives apparently reconciled to the presence of the white men, some of the chieftains continued to plot for their extermination. Opechancanough, now so old that he had to have an attendant at hand to lift his eyelids before he could see, once more gathered his warriors from out of the depths of the forests and gave the command for attack. Twenty-two years after the first massacre the warwhoop sounded again and the fury of the savages was unleashed upon the outlying plantations. Again the white men were caught off guard, again hundreds were slaughtered before effective resistance could be offered, again the terrified people came pouring in upon the older and more populous settlements.

At that time Sir William Berkeley, who had recently taken his seat as governor, acted with promptness and wisdom. Drawing the fugitives together in fortified camps, he struck back at the Indians vigorously and effectively. His expeditions drove them from their habitations, burnt their towns, destroyed their crops and inflicted heavy losses in killed and wounded. At last he overtook and captured "that bloody monster upon a hundred years old," Opechancanough, and brought him to Jamestown where he was killed by one of his guard. Soon after this the Indians, discouraged and starving, sued for peace and a treaty was concluded with the new "emperor" Necotowance. The conquered tribes acknowledged the King of England as their ruler, ceded all the land be-

THE INDIAN TERROR

tween the York and the James and put themselves under the protection of the white men.

Within the restricted area of their reservations the Indians now lived in comparative peace, planting their fields of maize, hunting in the dense woods and in the swamps, setting their traps for fish, making their dugout canoes, building their bark houses, gathering wild oats and "tuckahoe." The Indian who succeeded in accumulating a few furs or deer skins was fortunate, for he could bring them to Fort Henry or some other trading post to exchange for blankets, knives, cooking utensils and only too often for arms and ammunition.

For decades after 1644 the English remained suspicious of the neighboring tribes and kept a strict watch upon them, but so far from being a menace, they now constituted a very real protection against the attacks of other tribes. The Weyenoakes, Nottoways and Appomattox on the south, and the Chickahominies, Pamunkeys, Rappahannocks, Mattaponeys and other tribes on the west almost encircled the plantations and could furnish in case of need nearly a thousand fighting men. On one occasion, when a band of hostile Indians, possibly Mohawks, descended upon the upper James, the allied tribes fought side by side with Colonel Edward Hill's Virginians, and in the ensuing defeat lost many of their warriors, including their chief, Tottopottomoi. They were invaluable, also, as scouts for the white men, being as necessary "as dogs to hunt wolves," and as guides through the forests.

The year 1675 opened gloomily for the people of Virginia. There seemed to be some great disaster imminent, perhaps a pestilence, perhaps a devastating war. A great comet appeared in the sky, "streaming like a horsetail westwards" towards the horizon, and everyone knew how ominous that was. This was followed by a flight of pigeons in such numbers that they stretched as far as the eye could see, "whose weight broke down the limbs of large trees whereon they rested at night." This caused the older planters to shake their heads, for they remembered that a similar flight had preceded the massacre of 1644. As though this were not enough, vast swarms of insects "about an inch long and big as the top of a man's little finger" rose out of holes in the ground, and after eating the fresh leaves from the top of the trees, in a month's time disappeared.

The disaster, thus plainly indicated, broke in the north. On the banks of the Susquehanna River at the point where it crosses Mason and Dixon's Line lived the warlike Susquehannock Indians. George Alsop tells us that this tribe was regarded by the English "as the most noble and heroic nation of Indians" in all North America. Straight as arrows, of majestic carriage, proud and brave, they were dreaded by all the neighboring tribes. When going out to war they painted their faces, arms and breasts, smeared their hair with bear's grease, decorated their heads with swan feathers, stuck the tomahawk in their girdle and seized their guns, bows and arrows. As they passed out of their palisaded towns in troops of forty or more, they sang war songs praising the exploits of their ancestors. Returning with their hapless prisoners, they subjected them to unspeakable tortures—tearing off their scalps, heaping burning coals on their heads, searing their bodies with hot irons, cutting off strips of flesh.

The Susquehannocks had long been in alliance with the English of Maryland, upon whom they depended for assistance in their wars against the Senecas, one of the tribes of the Iroquois confederation. At the same time the Marylanders were glad enough to have six or seven

THE INDIAN TERROR

hundred fierce warriors as a barrier against the northern tribes, and so supplied the Susquehannocks with firearms and munitions. In 1674, however, Maryland made a separate treaty of peace with the Senecas, thus leaving their former allies to meet alone the fury of the ancient enemy.

Gallant, though they were, the Susquehannocks were no match for the Long House. They were defeated, swept out of their fortified towns and driven into Maryland to seek safety on the banks of the Patuxent. Even though they were now sixty or more miles from their former home they still had reason to dread the long arm of their enemies, and so moved on to the north bank of the Potomac just south of the Piscataway Creek.

In the meanwhile they sent Harignera and other leaders to St. Mary's to ask that some portion of Maryland be allotted them as their new place of residence. This request placed the Assembly in a quandary. If they permitted the Susquehannocks to remain near the plantations they might "corrupt" the nearby peaceable tribes and alienate them from the English, or the Senecas might follow them and thus embroil the colony in the war. On the other hand, the Susquehannocks still counted many fighters, so that to eject them by force might be difficult and costly. Finally it was decided to give them permission to occupy lands on the Potomac above the great falls. After "some tedious debate" the chieftains stated through their interpreter that "they would condescend" to accept this offer and leave their temporary quarters.

But weeks and months wore on and the Susquehannocks did not move. No doubt they realized that on the upper Potomac they would be as much exposed to the assaults of the Senecas as on the Susquehanna. For the moment they were sheltered by the proximity of the

Piscataways, whose protection they sought and whose fort might prove a refuge in time of peril. Yet their situation was desperate, for their food supply was low and the Piscataways would not want to share with them either their cornfields or their hunting grounds. They must either raid the English plantations or starve, and to rob the English would involve them in a war which must sooner or later be their ruin. When, then, various robberies were reported in the spring and early summer, both in Maryland and Virginia, the Susquehannocks were at once suspected.

One Sabbath morning, when certain good people of Stafford County on the Virginia side of the Potomac were on their way to church, they were horrified to find a certain Robert Hen lying across the threshold of his house desperately wounded with a dead Indian nearby. Although bleeding from ghastly wounds on his head, arms and body, poor Hen was able to gasp out "Doegs, Doegs," before he expired. A moment later a boy came out from his hiding place under a bed and stated that the murder had been committed by Indians. Now the Doeg Indians some years previously had been guilty of so many depredations and murders that the government of Virginia had proclaimed war upon them to be prosecuted "to their utter destruction." The people of Stafford were not surprised, therefore, that members of this hostile tribe, living on the Maryland side of the Potomac, had crossed over to renew the old outrages.

Immediately Colonel George Mason, commander of the Stafford infantry regiment, and Captain George Brent, of the horse, collecting thirty or more men, set out on the trail of the savages. Hastening up the river bank in the night until they were opposite the Indian reserva-

THE INDIAN TERROR

tion between the Piscataway and Mattawoman Creeks, they crossed over just at the break of dawn.

Upon landing on the Maryland shore and finding two paths in the woods leading in different directions, they divided their force, Mason leading one party and Brent the other. Brent had proceeded but a few hundred yards when he discovered an Indian cabin which he silently surrounded. Presently a Doeg chieftain emerged under pretense of holding a parley, but when he attempted to break through the ring of the English, Brent seized him by his hair and charged him with Hen's murder. The savage denied all knowledge of the crime and breaking away started to run, but Brent brought him down with a pistol shot. Thereupon the Doegs in the cabin, after firing a shot or two, thronged out of the door and fled in the face of a fusillade, leaving ten dead on the spot.

In the meanwhile Mason had also discovered a cabin a short distance away and stealthily surrounded it. The Indians within, alarmed at the sound of the firing, rushed out to be greeted by a volley which laid fourteen of them low. But in the midst of the fight an Indian came up to Mason shouting: "Susquehannocks, friends," and then fled into the woods. Thereupon Mason called out to his men: "For the Lord's sake shoot no more, these are our friends the Susquehannocks."

In this unfortunate affair Mason and Brent were seriously at fault. However indignant they might be at the murder of Hen, however necessary they considered it to discourage further depredations by a quick retaliation, they had no authority to invade a neighboring province and attack a group of Indians under the protection of the Maryland government. They could hardly have had proof that the savages in either of the cabins were the murderers they sought and so were merely trying to right one wrong with another. And, far from this expedition's putting an end to depredations by the Indians, it was sure to bring on a series of reprisals. So when the news spread through Stafford County on the Virginia side of the river and Charles County in Maryland of renewed murders, the people had good reason to curse the rashness of the two Virginians. In fact Governor Charles Calvert complained to Sir William Berkeley of "the intrusion of the Virginians on his province," to turn friendly Indians into deadly enemies, but this resulted in nothing more than ill will between the two colonies.

It became obvious, however, that the Virginians and Marylanders must stifle their mutual resentment in the face of the new peril. There could be no peace in either province with a band of infuriated savages encamped within a few miles of the plantations. Not only could they be expected to continue their isolated raids, but they might draw the Piscataways and other friendly Indians of the Potomac region into a hostile alliance and open a devastating war. So it was determined to raise a joint army of Virginians and Marylanders to force the Susquehannocks to withdraw from the region and perhaps to give hostages for their good conduct.

Now followed days of feverish preparation. As messengers rode through the Potomac counties summoning the militia to the colors, the planters dropped the hoe or the plow handle to take up the fusil, the sword, the halberd and the pistol. Barrels of wheat, corn and salt; casks of powder and shot; axes, nails, water casks, tents were assembled at the wharves, and there, amid the cursing and shouting of the captains and lieutenants, were rolled on board the waiting sloops. When the soldiers themselves had embarked and the sails were hoisted, the little fleet moved on up the Potomac. On the Maryland side the scene was equally martial, with the sounding of trumpets, the assembling of squadrons and the clatter of hoofs. The Maryland troops, under the command of Major Thomas Trueman, arrived on the site of Fort Washington on the north bank of Piscataway Creek on September 26, 1675, where they awaited the Virginians.

In the meanwhile the Susquehannocks had not been idle. Selecting an open bit of ground a few hundred feet from Mockley Point, where Piscataway Creek flows into the Potomac, they began the erection of a fort. At first sight this place would seem to have had little to recommend it, for it was dominated by the fort of the Piscataways, while the sloops of the English shut it in on two sides. The English anticipated no difficulty in taking the fortress.

Major Trueman's first step was to invite Harignera to come forth for a parley. But as Harignera was no longer living the Indians sent five other "great men" in his place. No doubt they were sincerely anxious to come to terms with the English, and were prepared to move to the site allotted them above the falls of the Potomac and perhaps give hostages for their good behavior. But Trueman immediately charged them with the recent murders in Maryland, especially with the attack upon the plantation of one Hanson. The chiefs replied that all the mischief had been done by prowling bands of Senecas, who since had withdrawn to the northward, but the angry Marylanders were not convinced and put them under guard.

The next day the Virginia troops, under the command of Colonel John Washington, grandfather of George Washington, and Colonel Isaac Allerton, of Northumberland, disembarked on the north bank of the creek. Immediately the five "great men" were brought before the two Virginians, who charged them, through an interpreter, with the murders in Stafford County. Again the Indians denied all, placing the blame on the Senecas. Why, said Washington and Allerton, we have witnesses to prove that several of the raiding parties came directly to your fort, their canoes laden down with our beef and pork. Is it likely that your enemies the Senecas would be so kind as to supply you with provisions? Moreover, some of your tribe have been seen on the Virginia side wearing the clothing of men recently murdered. Unless you can explain these matters we must account you enemies and proceed to storm your fort.

While this parley was in progress Major Trueman kept interrupting, asking: "Gentlemen are you finished? When you are done I will say something." So at last he turned to the captives and asked them how it happened, if the Senecas were the guilty ones, that the Indians killed at Hanson's should have been identified as Susquehannocks? When they once more denied complicity in the killings, Trueman ordered them to be bound, stating that he would take them to Hanson's so they themselves might view the bodies. Seeing himself in danger of death, one of the "great men" produced an old piece of paper and a medal with the image of Lord Baltimore on one side and that of Lady Baltimore on the other, to which was attached a black and yellow ribbon. This, he said was a pledge which a former governor of Maryland had given them, a token of friendship as long as the sun and the moon should last, which would always protect them from harm within the bounds of the province. But this availed them nothing. Trueman marched them off and before they had gone five hundred yards ordered his men to knock them on the head.

The blame for this breach of faith must rest on the shoulders of Major Trueman. It was he who invited the "great men" to the parley, it was he who murdered them. It is true that one of the Marylanders later stated that Colonel Washington approved of the executions, but the latter was able to show by several witnesses that Trueman acted on his own initiative, and that he had no intimation that the Indians were to be killed when they were led away. Had this not been so he and Allerton would certainly have felt the heavy hand of Sir William Berkeley, who was furiously angry when the news reached him. "If they had killed my grandfather and my grandmother, my father and mother and all my friends, yet if they had come to treat of peace, they ought to have gone in peace," he blurted out. Major Trueman was impeached by the lower House of the Maryland Assembly, found guilty by the upper House, fined and sentenced to imprisonment. The Council termed his deed "so great and unheard of a wickedness" that it was with difficulty that he could get his men to carry out his orders and that afterwards "not a man would own to have had a hand in it."

The murder of the chieftains was as stupid as it was treacherous, for it inspired the warriors in the fort to a desperate and successful defense. The fort itself was far stronger and more complex than the traditional Indian enclosure with its single circle of palisades, for the Marylanders themselves had given the Susquehannocks careful instruction in the art of fortification. Laying out a large square, they had raised high embankments on all four sides, with a ditch outside and high platforms or flankers at each corner. As an outer line of defense they made a palisade of trees from five to eight inches in diameter, sunk three feet in the earth, the tops twisted together and the spaces between the trunks large enough to serve as loopholes. Behind this formidable barrier the savages crouched and shouted their defiance.

A picturesque scene it was, this encounter between the natives of aboriginal America and the forces of the new civilization. As one stood upon the heights to the south the whole scene spread out as in a panorama—the broad Potomac with the wooded Virginia highlands beyond where a century later George Washington was to make his home; the Piscataway dotted with armed sloops; the Susquehannock fort enclosing a number of bark cabins; the redoubts of the English; the clusters of tents; the companies of cavalry maneuvering with glistening sabers; the foot bands under their pennants, formidable with their fusils and carbines.

The three commanders pitched camp on the hillside and then established their lines around the Indian stronghold. Had they been properly equipped with artillery they soon would have battered down the palisades and the platforms, but they seem to have had no heavy guns. Nor could they dig a mine beneath the fortifications to blow them up because of the marshy character of the ground. In perplexity they constructed a tower on wheels, the "mount" they called it, from which they could fire over the palisades into the fort, but this seems to have availed them little.

It would have been wiser to make their own lines as strong as possible and wait until starvation had forced the Indians to surrender. This should have been easy of accomplishment, for the armed sloops made escape in the canoes impossible, while a series of small marshes when linked together with redoubts should have put an effectual stop to sallies on the land side. But the English works were so badly constructed and their watch was so negligent that the savages repeatedly swarmed out, inflict-

THE INDIAN TERROR

ing severe losses, taking many of their fusils and spades and driving horses enough into their fort to supply themselves and families with food for many days.

All the while the fort was becoming stronger and stronger, so that at the end of seven weeks the English apparently were no nearer its capture than at the outset. When they suggested a parley, the savages asked bitterly: "Where are our great men?"

The Indians realized, however, that they could not remain indefinitely, so destroying everything which they could not carry off, they suddenly sallied out with their wives and children, broke through the lines of the besiegers and disappeared into the forest. Nothing was left for the English save to break camp and return to their homes, to give an account to their governments of their failure and their heavy losses.

The Virginians soon discovered that in permitting the Susquehannocks to escape they had opened Pandora's box. The enraged savages made their way up the left bank of the Potomac until they came to a ford, and, passing over to the Virginia side, fell upon the outlying plantations on the upper Rappahannock and Mattapony Rivers. Within a few days they had slaughtered sixty persons, men, women and children, and had spread terror through all the frontier region. Over and over again the same scene was enacted. There was the little frame cottage, the wife busy with her cooking or her sewing, the children playing nearby, the husband at work with his hoe in the field, and beyond the dark circle of the forest. Suddenly the warwhoop resounds, there is the sound of shots and a group of painted savages rush upon the unsuspecting family. In a few moments all is over and the Indians retire into the woods with scalps hanging at their belts, leaving the mutilated bodies to the vultures.

Yet the dead were fortunate as compared with those who were dragged away as captives. Deep in the forest, beyond hope of rescue, the savages subjected the wretched victims to the tortures of the damned. Binding their prisoners to stakes, they roasted them with slowly burning fires, cut strips of flesh from their bodies, tore their nails from their fingers. In wild terror the frontier settlers fled from their homes, bringing with them their families and what supplies they could transport, and leaving their houses and even their cattle to the mercy of the enemy. Sitterborne parish, on the frontier of Rappahannock County, lost thirty-six persons and "what with those who ran away" and those who "felt the fury of the enemy," was reduced from seventy-one plantations to eleven in less than three weeks.

As the fugitives poured down upon the more thickly settled regions, gasping out their stories of murders and tortures, and begging for protection, active preparations were made to defend the plantations. Encamped upon some of the larger farms, the fugitives were joined by the more exposed families of the neighborhood and set to work putting up palisades and making redoubts As soon as one place had been fortified, the neighbors in a body transferred their labors to the next. No man dared stir out of doors unarmed, sentinels were posted over those working in the fields.

In this crisis Sir William Berkeley at first showed a spark of the old resolution and decision which had made him so successful a leader in the former Indian war. Summoning his Council, he laid the situation before them and secured their approval for an expedition to follow the savages into the woods and take revenge for the recent atrocities. A force of horse and foot were assembled under the command of Sir Henry Chicheley, a soldier of experience who had served in the royal army in the English Civil War, with some of the leading planters of Rappahannock County to advise him. All was ready for the command to march, when, to the amazement and consternation of all, Berkeley suddenly decided not to pursue the Susquehannocks. Disbanding his forces, he left the frontiers without any adequate protection.

It is possible that it was the proffer of peace by the Indians at this juncture which was responsible for his strange conduct. The new chieftain reproached the Virginians for forgetting their promises of friendship, attacking his people even in another province and murdering the envoys of peace. But since he had now revenged himself by killing ten Virginians for one Susquehannock, if Berkeley would give compensation for his losses he was prepared to renew the old good relations. That Sir William sent a conciliatory reply and that he expected it to put an end to the murderous raids is indicated by Bacon's statement that he "gave his word for the peaceable demeanor" of the Indians.

The governor failed to realize that the situation had got out of hand for the chief himself. The Susquehannocks were now split into numerous small bands, each acting independently of the others, which were raiding the frontier both for revenge and to secure food. Some of the tribe had moved back to Maryland. The invaders seem also to have drawn in with them the disorderly elements of other tribes, some by force, others by the prospect of plunder. The Virginia frontiersmen were convinced that many from the allied tribes, the Pamunkeys, Chickahominies and others, were participating in the murders.

At all events, the only result of the peace negotiations was to throw Sir William off his guard, while fresh incursions on the outlying settlements, more destructive and brutal than ever, were in preparation. Had there been a flying force of English on the frontier to pursue the enemy at the first intimation of their presence, to overawe the tributary Indians and force them to ferret the invaders out of their hiding places and assist in their defeat, the war might have been brought to a speedy conclusion. But to leave the country unprotected, to permit the Susquehannocks to draw into their ranks every lawless savage within a circle of a hundred miles, was to undermine the traditional Indian policy of the colony, invite further murders, and bring down on the government the bitter complaints of the people.

In the meanwhile Sir William had summoned the Assembly, and on March 7, 1676, they gathered in the State House. This was the last session of the corrupt Long Assembly, and its policy in the Indian war was merely the reflection of Sir William's wishes. And the governor was still determined that there should be no expedition to pursue the invaders. Some of the people were now declaring openly that all Indians were alike and that all alike should be put to the sword. Berkeley seems to have feared that if a force were sent into the Indian country he might not be able to restrain the men from attacking the friendly tribes, burning their villages and driving them into the arms of the Susquehannocks. It would be better, he thought, to pursue a defensive policy, protect the plantations by a series of frontier forts, and trust to time and hunger to draw off the invaders.

So the Assembly declared war rather indefinitely upon all who were known "to have committed murders, rapines and depredations," enlisted five hundred soldiers, provided for the use of Indian allies, prohibited all trade in firearms with the savages, and ordered the erection of

THE INDIAN TERROR

forts on the frontiers in Stafford, at the falls of the Rappahannock, on the upper Mattapony, on the Pamunkey, at the falls of the James, at the falls of the Appomattox, in Surry and on the Nansemond. They then offered a reward of three coats of matchcloth to any allied Indian who would bring in an enemy, and of one coat for the head of every one killed, after which they humbly implored the divine assistance and blessing upon their endeavors and set aside two days for "public fasting and humiliation."

Once more Virginia was astir with martial preparations —the calling of men to the colors, the collecting of stores of beef, pork and corn, of shot and powder, of axes, hoes, spades, saws, wedges and nails; the loading of sloops and other boats and their departure for the upper reaches of the rivers. At the places designated for the forts all was activity and the Virginia forests resounded to the sound of the axe, the crash of falling trees and the shouts of busy men. No doubt there were eyes which peered out of the dark forest at these scenes and silent runners passing swiftly along almost impenetrable trails to report all that was going on to the various bands of hostile Indians. They knew just where each fort was located, how many men there were in the garrisons—and they knew that between the forts were miles of unprotected woods or swamps offering easy access to the heart of the colony.

The work on the forts had hardly begun when the terrifying news spread through the plantations of new raids, of butchered men and women, of wretched captives dragged away to be tortured. Some of these murders were committed in the more thickly settled parts of the colony, many miles within the circle of the forts, yet the Indians invariably retreated in safety. Even when some friendly Indian or a terrified planter came to one of the forts with information of the whereabouts of the Susquehannocks, the garrison could not pursue them until they had notified Governor Berkeley and received his permission. Long before they could hear from Sir William the opportunity had passed and the savages were perhaps fifty or more miles away, roasting their captives at their leisure.

Ere long a great hue and cry arose against the forts. Rather than pay the taxes for them, said the people, we will plant no more tobacco. "These useless structures are merely a new device to draw money out of the poor man's pockets." Does the governor imagine that the Indians are going to walk up to the walls of his forts so that the soldiers can shoot them down? Could he not foresee that they would come down upon our plantations where there are no forts, burning, plundering, murdering, almost without resistance? Our butchered wives, children and friends cry out to Heaven for revenge. After the great massacre of 1644 Sir William himself led the expeditions which hunted the savages out of their lairs and made them sue for peace. Why does he not pursue a similar course now? There are hundreds of sturdy men ready to follow him, who have enough English blood in their veins to prefer to die fighting than to be murdered in their beds by the sneaking enemy. If Sir William is too old to take the field, let him give one of our militia officers a commission to lead us out against the enemy and we will soon clear the woods of these savage villains.

In many a backwoods residence behind newly erected palisades angry men gathered to discuss the latest rumors of fresh bands of Indians assembling on the upper James for another descent on the plantations and to denounce the inactivity and stubbornness of the governor. All they asked, they said, was permission to defend themselves and their families, and surely Sir William could not deny them that. So, in one county after another, petitions were drawn up asking the governor to send them a leader with orders to go out against the enemy. As the Charles City delegation, after presenting their petition to the irritable old man, stood humbly before him, one of them happened to speak of themselves as his honor's subjects. Why, you are a set of "fools and loggerheads," blurted out the governor. "You are the King's subjects and so am I." Get out and a "pox take you." Soon after this the sheriffs in the various counties were directed to tack on the courthouse doors a proclamation forbidding petitions of this kind in the future.

If Nathaniel Bacon absented himself from the Council meetings in the fall and winter of 1675-1676, as seems likely, only vague rumors must have come to him of the Indian depredations on the upper Potomac, the assembling of the army before the Susquehannock fort, the murder of the "great men" and the escape of the Indians. To a planter in Henrico, Piscataway Creek was almost as far away as New Amsterdam or London.

But the news of the raids upon the upper Rappahannock, with all the ghastly details of murders and tortures, spread through the backwoods like wildfire. No doubt Bacon had heard much about the Indians during his brief sojourn in the colony, and he must have seen many of them at William Byrd's trading post near his own plantation at the falls of the James. The vivid details of their cruelty now aroused the deepest loathing and resentment. Men who had spent their lives in Virginia knew that the Indians when not aroused had their good qualities, and many had received kindnesses from them and perhaps had formed attachments among them. But to Bacon they were the demons they showed themselves when warring on defenseless women and children. He must have shuddered at the thought of a group of painted warriors descending on Curles Neck, shooting down his servants, killing his little daughter and dragging Elizabeth off into captivity.

His heart was moved, also, by the plight of the people. It was enough that they should be impoverished by Parliament, betrayed by their own representatives in the Assembly, tyrannized over by the governor and burdened with taxes, but to be left defenseless against the raids of the savages, even deprived of the privilege of defending themselves, was the last straw. When he heard that Berkeley had again refused to grant permission for an Indian expedition he swore that, commission or no commission, the next time a murder was committed he would go out against them, though no more than twenty men volunteered to follow him. This I considered my duty, Bacon said afterwards, for since the governor placed me here in a position of trust I thought it my duty to look after the welfare of the people, they being poor, few and in scattered habitations on the frontier.

He did not have long to wait, for news came of an attack on the settlements at the falls of the James, accompanied by the usual atrocities. This time the blow struck home to Bacon himself, for the Indians killed his overseer "of whom he was very fond," laid waste his upper plantation, spoiled his crop of tobacco and robbed him of a large part of his cattle. Again the terrified people fled before the enemy, leaving their houses and cattle and provisions a "prey to the enemy," to seek refuge in the more thickly settled neighborhoods where they "were crowded together like sheep" and became dependent upon charity for their food. Upon this "I sent to the governor for a commission," Bacon tells us, "but being from time to time denied . . . and finding the lives and fortunes of the poor inhabitants wretchedly sacrificed, resolved to stand up in this ruinous gap and rather expose my life and fortune to all hazards than basely desert my post."

At this juncture word spread through Henrico and Charles City Counties that the hostile Indians had formed themselves into several formidable bodies fifty or sixty miles above the falls of the James and were coming down for a new assault. The terrified people, deserted by their government, began to assemble in arms for their own protection. Men went from plantation to plantation beating drums and calling for volunteers, and the various groups assembled on the south side of James River at Jordan's Point near Merchants Hope, almost opposite the site of Westover. A strange scene they presented—poor farmers in ragged homespun, frontiersmen in buckskin, well-to-do planters who held high office under the government, all armed with fusils, carbines, swords and pistols, and provided with provisions and pack horses for the march through the woods. On all sides there were bitter denunciations of the governor, curses at the useless forts and determination to go into the forest to hunt the savages out of their hidden lairs.

They waited only for a leader and this leader, they hoped, would be Bacon. Captain James Crews of Turkey Island had led them to expect that Bacon would accept the post. He was known to be "popularly inclined," a friend of the people and in sympathy with their protests against the lack of adequate protection against the Indians and the unjust "impositions laid on them." At the moment Bacon was on the north side of the river, probably at "Doggans," the plantation of Henry Isham, in company with Isham, Crews and William Byrd. As usual the topic of conversation was the "sadness of the times," the pall of dread that hung over men's heads, the desolation already created by the Indians, the stubbornness of the governor. Thereupon it was suggested that they all row over the river to visit the forces at Jordan's Point.

When the little party landed the volunteers pressed around them and someone shouted: "Bacon! Bacon!" Immediately the cry: "Bacon! Bacon! Bacon!" was taken up and resounded from a hundred throats. His friends joined in the general acclaim and urged him to take command of the army and so rescue the colony from the Indian horror. They would all place themselves under his leadership, they declared, would follow him into the forest; they drank "damnation to their souls" should they be false to him. So, to the great joy of the soldiers, the young man was persuaded to accept.

A momentous decision it was. Bacon himself could not know that a century later a similar decision was to be made when the Massachusetts minutemen rushed to Lexington to defend their liberties with arms in their hands. He had no way of foreseeing that another Virginian would some day head an army which, like the little band who stood cheering around him, was to fight for the right of Americans to govern themselves. Perhaps he had not considered the possibility of independence or reasoned that the acts of Parliament discriminating against the colonies might one day make it inevitable. He was merely striking out blindly against injustice and oppression. But in so doing he sounded a warning, not only to Sir William Berkeley, but to the King, that Americans would not hesitate to fight for the liberties which they had inherited and which the freedom of life on the frontier had made doubly dear.

THE INDIAN TERROR

It is possible that had there been no Indian war the Virginians would not have risen against the governor, but, having taken arms in defense of their lives, they seized the opportunity to defend their liberties as well. Bacon promised his followers not only to fight the Indians, but to redress their many grievances—the unjust laws, the oppressive taxes, the corruption of their representatives, the favoritism shown by the courts. The governor he denounced "as negligent and wicked, treacherous and incapable," whose selfishness, stubbornness and love of power had impoverished the people and left them at the mercy of the savages.

Instantly Bacon became the popular hero. If formerly the poor planters had loved him because of his sympathy for their sufferings, they now adored him as their one hope, "the only patron of the country and preserver of their lives and fortunes." In every humble home from one end of the colony to the other the news spread that a popular leader had arisen, one who did not cringe before the governor and who dared to denounce his tyranny and to promise redress even by force of arms.

So the little army at Jordan's Point took an oath "to stick fast together" and be true to Bacon, and signed their names "circular wise that their ringleaders might not be found out."

The immediate concern, of course, was the Indian expedition. From out the forest, by some mysterious means of communication, had come the information that a large group of Susquehannocks had gone south to the Roanoke River, not far from Occaneechee Island near the North Carolina border. It was at this spot that the Occaneechee Indians, under their chieftain Rossechy, or Persicles, had fortified themselves directly athwart the great southwest trading path. Here came traders from the Cherokees and other tribes of the southwest with their beaver furs and deer skins; here came the pack trains of Abraham Wood and other Virginia merchants, with guns, shot, hatchets, kettles, blankets, knives and trinkets. The Occaneechees tried to prevent either group from passing, so that they themselves might act as middlemen and make a profit both from the southern Indians and the Virginians. The Occaneechee trail led northeast from the island and crossing the Meherrin and the Nottoway Rivers, terminated at Fort Henry at the falls of the Appomattox. Connecting with this trail was another path leading to William Byrd's trading post at the falls of the James. Over these thread-like forest highways travelled long caravans of horses, sometimes numbering fifty or more, and each carrying packs of from one hundred and fifty to two hundred pounds, under the charge of fifteen or sixteen men.

After visiting New Kent County to recruit his forces and perhaps pausing at Curles Neck to say goodbye to Elizabeth, Bacon with his determined band plunged into the forest. They headed first not towards the Roanoke, but the Nottoway River, for Bacon wished to swell his numbers with some sturdy warriors from the friendly Nottoways and Meherrins. With this in mind they turned southward, no doubt over the trail discovered in 1650 by Abraham Wood and Edward Bland.

A picturesque scene it was, this band of Virginians, making their way along the narrow path beaten hard by the feet of thousands of Indians and perhaps by untold numbers of buffalo before them, through the woods fragrant with the spring wild flowers. Now they had to cross shallow creeks, now they passed open spaces where at some former time the Indians had had a field of maize, now they were enshrouded in the dense woods, now they

THE INDIAN TERROR

crossed pleasant meadows, now they had to wade knee deep through a broad river, now they skirted a swamp.

The Nottoway fort and town, situated on the Nottoway River south of the falls of the Appomattox, was typical of the Virginia Indian villages. The palisaded wall, about ten feet high and leaning slightly outwards, enclosed several rows of cabins formed of saplings bent into arches and covered with bark. No doubt Bacon and his men were welcomed with the usual war dances by painted warriors, who sang and kept time with their heads and arms to the beating of a drum formed by stretching a skin over a large gourd. But the Nottoways were not forward in offering assistance, and Bacon seems to have gone on some miles further to get what men he could from the Meherrins. The Meherrins too were reluctant to risk their lives in a war with the Susquehannocks, and Bacon secured in all only twenty-four warriors while he wearied his men with long marches and drew heavily upon his slender store of provisions.

He now retraced his steps until he came once more to the Occaneechee trail and then headed southwest upon it for the Roanoke. But his provisions were growing dangerously short, he still had many miles to go and he permitted some of his followers to turn back to their homes. When at last he reached the Roanoke there remained with him only seventy men and food sufficient for three days. The weary men emerged from the forest to find themselves looking out over the river about 240 feet to an island several miles long. Upon the high ground in the center surrounded by fields of maize, peach orchards and great forest trees, were three forts, with naked Indian children playing nearby and squaws going in and out of bark cabins. On the north bank a number of canoes manned by sturdy warriors were waiting for them, so they clambered in and were paddled over to the island, where they pitched camp and opened negotiations with Rossechy.

Bacon had already received intelligence that a party of thirty Susquehannock warriors with their wives and children had built a fort not far from the island. With them were a number of Indians of other tribes who had been forced to join in the raids on the plantations, among them some Mannikins whose village on the Pamunkey River had long been under the protection of the English. These unwilling allies assured Bacon by a secret messenger that they would be ready to assist him in his attack on the Susquehannocks. The Occaneechees, also, could have no love for the intruders whose war upon the English had brought about the prohibition of the fur and skin trade which had been the basis of their prosperity. So it was agreed, apparently, that Rossechy should lead his warriors out against the Susquehannock fort, and at a given signal assault it from without while the Mannikins and other captive Indians fell on the warriors from within.

This plan worked to perfection. Taken by surprise, the Susquehannocks made little resistance, so that those who were not killed were taken prisoners and brought in triumph to Occaneechee Island. The English must have rejoiced to see the fierce warriors who had committed such fiendish cruelties brought back as captives to await execution. But even their desire for revenge could not keep them from turning away in disgust as the Occaneechees put them to death "after their way," with all the excruciating tortures their ingenuity could devise.

Despite the destruction of the Susquehannocks, Bacon's position was critical. Practically without food, surrounded by savages of questionable friendship, eighty

THE INDIAN TERROR

miles or more from the nearest settlement, his men fast deserting him to return home, fearing that a sudden rain would make it difficult to bring the horses across the river, he was in danger both of starvation and of being cut off by the Indians. Had Rossechy supplied him with food for the return journey it is probable that he would have left the island satisfied with what had been accomplished. But now the Occaneechees and the Mannikins began to take a hostile attitude, kept close guard upon their provisions, and began manning the forts.

Philip Ludwell later accused Bacon of precipitating the break by demanding that the Occaneechees surrender the Mannikins to him together with the spoils taken from the Susquehannock fort. It is quite possible that some of Bacon's men had recognized among the Mannikins individuals who had participated in the attacks on the plantations. When they pointed out this warrior or that as the savage who had scalped a neighbor or murdered an entire family or plundered a plantation, it would be difficult not to demand his surrender. At the same time the fact that the Indians from many miles around had been accustomed to resorting to the Occaneechees for arms and ammunition makes it possible that Bacon deliberately picked a quarrel in order to put an end to the traffic. But Ludwell was bitterly hostile to Bacon and his statement is too obviously colored to be taken at its face value. It must be remembered that the English were forced to defend themselves because Rossechy marshalled all of his warriors together with the visiting braves, put his forts in a posture of defense, and posted strong bodies of men on the north bank of the river to cut off escape.

As the situation became more threatening, the Indians in the cabins outside the fort, men, women and children, tried to rush in through the gates, but Bacon interposed his men and held them all as hostages. At this moment, when all was suspense, a shot rang out and one of the English fell dead. Instantly Bacon gave the order to attack and his men, rushing up to the palisades around the forts, began firing in at the portholes. A hideous din arose, the howling and singing of the Indians and the groans of the dying mingling with the reports of the guns. While some of the English were thus occupied, others fell upon the hostages and slew them all. Still others managed to set fire to one of the forts in which were the chief and his family, so that many perished in the flames. Some of the braves made a dash for safety through the English, but were greeted with so deadly a volley that only four made good their escape.

The next day the fight continued from dawn until night, the savages from time to time sallying out and firing at the English from behind trees. But Bacon had posted his men so artfully that the Indians could find no shelter, and many were shot down "behind trees as they stood." At last in desperation the chief with twenty of his men rushed out into the neighboring fields, and running in a circle around the English, tried to pick them off. One by one they fell before the fire of Bacon's men until, when Rossechy himself was killed, the others sought safety in flight. The remnant of the Occaneechees, discouraged at the loss of their chief, with one of their forts destroyed and many of their warriors killed, gathering around them their women and children and pushing off in their canoes, made good their escape.

This was a great victory indeed, and Bacon was well satisfied with the results of his campaign. He had brought about the annihilation of a large body of Susquehannocks, had wiped out the Occaneechee trading post, killed three chieftains and a hundred warriors and brought off

THE INDIAN TERROR

a number of prisoners. And what he "reckoned most material," he had turned the Indians against each other and left them engaged in a "civil war." He could not be sure that his victory would put an end to the attacks on the plantations, for there were other bands of hostile savages at large who would take advantage of the disrupted times to satisfy their appetite for rapine. But he had struck a severe blow at the chief disturbers of the peace, had made it difficult for others to secure arms, and had demonstrated that the English were capable of revenging their injuries.

So it was with a spirit of elation that the young leader gathered his men around him there on the island amid the smoldering ruins of the Indian villages and with the dead still lying unburied upon the ground, to ask whether they wished to return home. Weary and faint with hunger though they were, the men would have followed Bacon through the forests for another expedition had he given the word. But since all were satisfied with what had been accomplished, they assembled their prisoners, gathered up their spoils, swam their horses over the river and set their faces towards the plantations.

CHAPTER IV
BATTLES ON THE JAMES

"MARS AND MINERVA BOTH IN HIM CONCURRED"

Battles on the James

WHEN BERKELEY HEARD THAT BACON HAD DEFIED HIM and was making active preparations for the Indian expedition, he was infuriated. How dared this young man of twenty-nine, a newcomer in the colony, pit his judgment against one who had ruled Virginia for decades and had acquired his knowledge of Indian affairs by long experience? How dared he show contempt for the royal authority reposed in the governor and place himself at the head of an armed force bent not only on attacking the savages but on forcing important reforms from the government.

Before resorting to force he issued a proclamation granting a pardon to Bacon and his followers provided they lay down their arms immediately and "return to their duty and allegiance." When this had no effect, he sent out a call for troops for an expedition to Henrico to intercept Bacon and prevent his march against the Indians. In all the adjacent counties the leading planters seized their swords and their carbines and rode to Middle Plantation, the site of Williamsburg, to place themselves under the governor's command. On May 3, when three hundred had assembled, the bugles sounded, the men mounted and clattered away through the plantations of Charles City and the woods of Henrico to the falls of the James.

But they were too late. The frontiersmen had already crossed the river and were hastening south through the forest. One wonders what would have been the outcome had Bacon waited to meet the governor and the two forces had clashed there on the site of Richmond. Would the "commoners," the forerunners of the minutemen of a century later, led by the youthful patriot, have withstood the assaults of Berkeley's troop of gentlemen, bent on upholding the existing order? It is probable that Bacon's men, with their superior skill in firearms and their knowledge of the ground, and with the resolution born of years of injustice, would have overwhelmed their opponents, perhaps have captured the governor and made themselves masters of Virginia at one blow.

Since Berkeley could not close in on Bacon with his armed forces he had to content himself with hurling after him every legal thunderbolt in his power:

Nathaniel Bacon, junior, of Henrico County, with divers rude, dissolute and tumultuous persons, contrary to the laws of England and their allegiance to the King, have taken arms without obtaining from me any order or commission, he declared in a proclamation dated May 10. Since this tends to the ruin and overthrow of the government, I do declare that he and his aiders are unlawful, mutinous and rebellious. I suspend Bacon from the Council of State, his office of justice of the peace and from all other offices civil and military, since his rash, headstrong and unlawful proceedings prove that he is unfit for any such trust. It is amazing that after I have been in Virginia for thirty-four years, most of the time as governor, have done equal justice to all men and in former Indian wars met with great success, any of the people should be so easily seduced by so young, inexperienced and rash a person as Nathaniel Bacon. Yet I hereby grant free pardon to all his followers, save John Sturdivant and Thomas Willford, the chief promoters of this rebellion, provided they all depart from Bacon and return to their homes and continue faithful and obedient.

For poor Elizabeth Bacon this was a time of cruel anxiety. She feared that her husband, many miles away in the mysterious Virginia forest, would fall a victim to the tomahawk or the scalping knife, or perhaps give up his life amid the tortures of the stake. Yet she dreaded to have him come back lest he fall into the clutches of the vindictive governor. Berkeley had gone out of his way to visit Curles Neck to tell her "that he would most certainly hang him as soon as he returned." "I pray God to keep the worst enemy I have from ever being in such a sad condition as I," she wrote to Nathaniel's sister, Elizabeth. "If you had been here, it would have grieved your heart to hear the pitiful complaints of the people, the Indians killing the people daily and the governor not taking any notice of it for to hinder them. The poor people came to your brother," and when the governor would not grant him a commission he went out against the Indians without one. "What for fear of the governor's hanging him and what for fear of the Indians killing him," she was quite distracted.

In the meanwhile Berkeley was very active on the frontier, probably hoping in this way to still the bitter criticisms of his former negligence. He rode through the upper James River region, visiting the fort on the Pamunkey and sending out scouting parties to locate bodies of Indians, friendly or hostile. The Pamunkey village he found deserted. The Queen of the Pamunkeys, the widow of Tottopottomoi, knowing either that some of her warriors had joined the Susquehannocks in their attacks on the English or that the suspicions of the frontiersmen were directed towards her, had withdrawn her people to the Dragon Swamp, at the head of Piankitanck River, where they had fortified themselves. There a party led by Colonel Claiborne visited her and commanded her to return to her reservation. But the Queen replied that she dared not do so, for since Sir William could not protect himself against Bacon he could not protect her. Yet she would remain peaceable in her new retreat, she said, giving no assistance to the Susquehannocks nor to any other tribe hostile to the English.

Berkeley was preparing to march against the Queen when he was forced to turn back by the alarming news that the people in various parts of the colony were rising in arms. Angry and sullen because of the restrictions on their trade, the levying of heavy taxes for the useless forts and Berkeley's arbitrary rule, they were preparing to march to the rescue of the young leader who was risking his life to rid the colony of the Indian menace.

Berkeley was greatly alarmed. If he yielded nothing to the popular clamor the colony would soon be in a blaze, and Bacon, when he returned, would be its dictator as well as hero. So he dissolved the old Assembly and issued writs for an election of burgesses, not by the freeholders alone as formerly, but by all freemen. "Finding by the too frequent complaints that the so long continuance of the present Assembly is looked upon as a grievance," he said in a proclamation, although he must testify to the ability and services of the present burgesses, yet to satisfy the people he did most regretfully dissolve them. And they were to repair to the usual voting places to elect as their burgesses two of the "most sage" persons in each county. "All persons are to have liberty freely to present to the said burgesses all such just complaints as they or any other have against me as governor. . . . And supposing I who am head of the Assembly may be the greatest grievance, I will most gladly join with them in a petition to his Majesty to appoint a new governor of Virginia, and thereby to ease and discharge me from the great care and trouble thereof in my old age."

But Berkeley remained firm in his determination to intercept Bacon and put him on trial as a rebel. Sending back his most influential supporters in each county to disperse the armed bands, and restore quiet and bring pressure for the election of burgesses well affected to the governor, he remained at the fort at the falls of the James with a part of his original forces now augmented by the garrison. But after watching the terminus of the Indian path for several weeks like a cat waiting for a mouse to emerge from its hole, he received word from certain members of the Council that his presence was necessary at the opening of the Assembly. So, reluctantly breaking camp, he rode back to his residence at Green Spring.

Hardly had he gone when Bacon's little band, half-starved, their clothing torn by the underbrush, wearied by long marching and fighting, returned from the Occaneechee expedition.

When the news of their victory spread from plantation to plantation, Bacon became more than ever the popular hero. Elizabeth was overjoyed at his safe return and filled with pride at the people's affection. "The country does so really love him," she wrote proudly to his sister, "that they would not leave him alone anywhere; there was not anybody against him but the governor and a few of his great men which have got their estates by the governor. Surely if your brother's crime had been so great all the country would not have been for him. . . . I do verily believe that rather than he should come to hurt . . . they would willingly lose their lives." Fearing that the governor might send troops to arrest him, Bacon's men kept constant vigil at his house and accompanied him wherever he went.

The indignation of the men who had gone out against the Indians knew no bounds when they learned that Berkeley had proclaimed them rebels and traitors. Some of the leaders, acting as spokesmen, drew up a paper of vindication explaining their motives in terse, vigorous phrases. They spoke of the terror caused by the Indian murders, of the exposed condition of the frontier, of the uselessness of the forts. Still having "so much English blood in us as to account it far more honorable to adventure our lives in opposing them . . . to the last drop of our blood, than to be sneakingly murdered by them in our beds," they appealed to the governor to empower them to resist. They continued: When his honor refused our request we would have submitted had the Indians ceased attacking us. But they continued to murder our relatives and friends, whose blood cried aloud to Heaven, while news reached us of "divers hundreds more of them coming down upon us." What a strait we were in, between submitting to the governor on the one hand, and need for protection on the other. What flesh could endure to lie still until we were destroyed by the heathen on pain of being accounted rebels and traitors. Although we cannot deny that we have vented our discontents in complaints of other grievances also, too great to be wholly smothered, we declare that our taking up arms was purely intended to preserve our very beings and not to relieve ourselves by the sword from any pressure in government.

In the meanwhile Berkeley sent word to Bacon to lay down his arms and come at once to Jamestown to answer for his disobedience. But in view of the governor's threats to hang him, Bacon hesitated to place himself at his

BATTLES ON THE JAMES

mercy, and continued to rely for protection on the fusils of his devoted followers. So finally, on May 29, Berkeley issued another proclamation which he ordered read at every courthouse in the colony, again denouncing Bacon as a rebel.

A few days later an exciting scene was enacted at Varina. It was election day and scores of planters from many miles around had assembled before the tiny courthouse to do their part in returning a House of Burgesses which Berkeley could neither bribe nor intimidate. Inside, where the justices were sitting, the sheriff rose and began reading the latest proclamation, when Bacon entered followed by about forty armed men and forced him to surrender the paper. As for the election, there had never been a doubt of the result. Bacon, the people's friend and their deliverer from the Indians, who was not afraid to oppose the old governor and expose his tyranny, was to be the representative of Henrico in the new Assembly. With him was chosen his friend and staunch supporter, Captain James Crews.

But the frontiersmen would not permit Bacon to put his head in the lion's mouth by going down to Jamestown unattended. When he bade goodbye to his little family and stepped on board his sloop, forty armed men took their places beside him. The youthful patriot must have had many misgivings as the craft made its way around the Turkey Island bend and headed down stream towards Jamestown. Perhaps it was rash to attempt to take his seat in the Assembly while under indictment as a rebel; perhaps it would have been wise to come unattended by armed men. But he was determined to champion the people's cause in the Virginia "House of Commons" by demanding the repeal of unjust laws and proposing reforms long overdue, and he could not hang back out of fear for his personal safety.

On June 6 the sloop, with its picturesque group, came abreast of Jamestown and cast anchor, while a messenger rowed ashore to inquire of the governor whether Bacon and Crews might take their seats without molestation. For answer they received a volley from the "great guns" in the brick fort, which made them hoist sail and hurry further up the river. But when they were veiled by the darkness of night Bacon with some of his men came ashore and, unobserved by the guard, made their way to the residence of Richard Lawrence across the main road from the State House. Here he held a conference with Lawrence and Drummond who gave him the latest news of the governor's intentions concerning himself, of the character of the new Assembly and what steps were being taken to prevent the passage of liberal legislation. He then slipped away to his boat and regained the sloop in safety.

The next morning Bacon turned his prow homeward and started up the river pursued by a number of armed boats. He probably would have made his escape had they not forced him under the guns of the ship *Adam and Eve*, commanded by Captain Thomas Gardiner. Seeing resistance useless, Bacon and his men surrendered and coming on board, were brought back to Jamestown as prisoners. Great indeed was the excitement in the little capital, now crowded with councillors, burgesses and others attracted by the meeting of the Assembly, as the youthful patriot and his sullen followers stepped ashore and were led before the governor.

"Now I behold the greatest rebel that ever was in Virginia," exclaimed the old man, raising his arms above his head. To this Bacon made no reply but stood with bowed head and dejected look.

After a short pause Berkeley spoke again: "Mr. Bacon have you forgot to be a gentleman?"

"No, may it please your honor," Bacon replied.

"Then, I'll take your parole." For this unexpected leniency Bacon expressed his gratitude and then withdrew. But his followers who had been captured with him were kept in irons awaiting trial.

It was probably the evening of the same day that Nathaniel Bacon, senior, sought out his cousin for a long and earnest conversation. In many ways the elder Bacon was the exact opposite of the younger. A self-made man who had won his position by ability, prudence and hard work, he regarded Nathaniel's defiance of the governor as headstrong folly which would not only bring about his own ruin but would fail to accomplish any good for the colony. He seems to have had a real affection for his cousin and perhaps an unconscious admiration for his hatred of injustice, his frankness and his bravery. So now he pleaded earnestly with him to make his submission to the governor and give up his plans for reforming the government and going out again without a commission to fight the Indians. I am growing old, he said, I have no children, it is my wish that you be my heir. If you will live quietly I will turn over to you at once a considerable part of my estate and leave you the remainder after my own and my wife's death.

At length Nathaniel yielded. He was in the governor's power and he knew that the enraged old man would not hesitate to hang him. No doubt the frontiersmen would swarm down to Jamestown to save him, but they might arrive too late. So when his cousin drew up a full submission, with a promise to do his best to "allay those great commotions which now grew high and fierce" and "engaged his estate and honor" to refrain from further disobedience to the government, he finally affixed his signature.

This was welcome news to Governor Berkeley. He knew that Bacon was the idol of the people and that his arrest would infuriate them and probably drive them into open rebellion. He had information that hundreds of armed men were already on their way to Jamestown, making threats to "double revenge all wrongs that should be done to Mr. Bacon or his men." Already angry groups were to be seen on the State House green or on Back Street, and their menacing looks warned Berkeley of what he had to expect. So, restraining his desire to revenge himself on his youthful rival, whom he despised as a popular upstart, he set the scene for submission and forgiveness.

One morning shortly after, while the burgesses were in session in the Long Room of the State House, the governor summoned them to a joint meeting with the Council. So they clattered down the stairs and filing into the General Court room below, waited to see what was wanted. Presently Berkeley stood up, saying: "If there be joy in the presence of the angels over one sinner that repenteth, there is joy now, for we have a penitent sinner come before us. Call Mr. Bacon."

Whereupon Nathaniel stepped forward and falling upon one knee, handed in his submission and promise of good behavior. There was a short pause. Then the governor resumed: "God forgive you! I forgive you! God forgive you! I forgive you! God forgive you! I forgive you!"

Colonel William Cole, from his seat in the Council, spoke up: "And all that were with him?"

"Yes, and all that were with him," replied the governor.

Once more there was silence for perhaps a minute. Then the governor, "starting up" from his chair a third time, said: "Mr. Bacon, if you will live civilly but till next Quarter Court, I will promise to restore you again to your place there," pointing to his seat in the Council. After this the burgesses withdrew. But Bacon did not have to wait till the next Quarter Court for his restoration. The afternoon of the same day, one of the burgesses on the way to the Long Room above, looked in through the door of the Council Chamber and saw Bacon seated in his accustomed place with the governor and the other members of the Council. "Which seemed a marvellous indulgence to one whom he had so lately proscribed a rebel."

But there was cool reason, not generosity, behind the indulgence. Berkeley had much less to fear from Bacon as a member of the Council than as a burgess. So long as he had him at his right hand, he could make no fiery speeches to the representatives of the people, point out the injustice of the taxes, propose reforms in local government, protest against the closing of the best land to poor settlers by great grants to favorites. If his hatred of oppression now and then got the better of him and made him blurt out his protests in the Council meetings, it would result in nothing more serious than a rebuke from the governor and the frowns of his cousin, of Cole, Ludwell, Ballard and the others. In other words, it was as good strategy now as it had been when Bacon was first appointed to the Council, to commandeer the leader of the popular movement as a member of the governor's official family.

That Bacon was greatly needed in the new House of Burgesses soon became evident. The burgesses, elected under the wider franchise and reflecting the discontent of the country, were earnestly desirous of reform. No sooner had they taken their seats and Berkeley had warned them to beware of being misled by the "two rogues" Lawrence and Drummond, both dwelling in Jamestown, than the question of redress of grievances was taken up. One member moved for an investigation of the handling of public revenues, another wanted the collectors' accounts examined. But at this juncture a pressing message came from the governor "to meddle with nothing until the Indian business had been dispatched." And though some were for disobeying and the "debate rose high," and though the poor people "groaned" at the friends of reform being thus overborne, no investigation of corruption in the handling of funds was made.

So the House proceeded to appoint a committee on Indian affairs. When one of Berkeley's henchmen proposed that they request the governor to send two members of the Council to sit with this body, the burgesses sat silent "looking at each other with many discontented faces." It was to be the old story over again, the "committee must submit to being overawed," and any spirit of opposition frowned down and reported to the governor.

Thomas Mathews suggested that the committee meet alone to draw a plan of operations against the Indians in accordance with the views of the House, and then, if the governor and Council did not approve, to have a joint consultation. This caused an uproar and one member remarked that it had always been customary to join some of the councillors to committees of this kind. Whereupon,

William Presley, of Northumberland, rose and said in a blunt, homely way: "'Tis true it has been customary, but if we have any bad customs we have come here to mend them." Despite the laughter which this occasioned, Berkeley had his way and two councillors were joined to the committee.

That the governor had not changed his views as to the proper method of combatting the Indian raids is shown by his efforts to bring the Pamunkeys back to their reservation and to enlist their aid against the Susquehannocks.

When the committee on Indian affairs met in the Hall of the Burgesses, the Queen of the Pamunkeys was ushered into the room, on her left hand her son of twenty, on her right an English interpreter. A striking figure she made, with her graceful, dignified bearing and her picturesque costume. She wore a mantle of deerskins, the hair outward and the edge cut into a fringe six inches deep, which reached from her shoulders to her feet, while upon her head was a crown of black and white wampum. "With grave courtlike gestures and a majestic air in her face," she walked up the Long Room to the end of the committee table, where she sat down.

The chairman asked her how many men she would lend for guides and fighters against the hostile tribes. After some "musing with an earnest passionate countenance, as if tears were ready to gush out," she made a short address in her native tongue, often repeating the words "Tottopottomoi chepiank." It was whispered around the table that she was reproaching the English because her husband, Tottopottomoi, and many of his warriors had been slain while fighting as allies of the English, for which no compensation had been made to her and her people.

The only reply which the chairman made to these reproaches was to demand brusquely: "What Indians will you now contribute?"

The Queen gave him a reproachful look and then turning her head, sat mute.

When the same question had been repeated for the second time, she replied in a low voice: "Six."

When this did not satisfy the chairman, she said: "Twelve," and "so rose up and gravely walked away."

Now followed several busy days in which the committee drew up their plans for prosecuting the war. The tributary Indians were to be brought back to their former towns and called upon to assist in trailing and attacking hostile bands; an army of one thousand men, including one hundred and twenty-five horse, were to be raised and sent to the frontiers; orders were issued for the collecting of arms, ammunition, provisions, medicines and other stores. As a sop to the people it was decided to abandon the useless forts in Henrico, New Kent and Rappahannock, and to distribute their garrisons among fourteen frontier plantations.

Yet the people were far from being satisfied. Is not this the old costly plan under a new guise, they asked? Does it propose any practical way of preventing the so-called friendly Indians from joining our enemies? Does it provide for a volunteer army to pursue the savages into the forest? No. It merely increases our burdens by raising an army which will be powerless to protect us. When Bacon's friends were gathering in Jamestown to rescue him from the governor, they had been induced to return home not only by the news of his pardon, but by a promise from one of Berkeley's friends in the Assembly that he would have his commission as general in the Indian war.

BATTLES ON THE JAMES

So now the poor farmers and especially the frontiersmen began to demand that this promise be fulfilled.

As the days passed Bacon began to become restless. He found himself muzzled and helpless, while things were carried on in the old high-handed way—the burgesses overawed, the plans for reform set aside, the Indian war mismanaged. Some of Bacon's friends began to whisper that his life was still in danger and that the purpose of the new army was more to prevent an uprising in the colony than to fight the Indians. As he sat in his seat in the Council, listening to the governor's plans and witnessing his overbearing conduct, he must have thought of himself as a traitor to the plain people.

In the end he determined to escape. Approaching Berkeley he told him he had received news that his wife was ill and requested permission to pay her a visit at Curles. When the governor, with grave misgivings, told him he might go, he mounted his horse and rode quietly out of town unaccompanied by servants or friends.

Hardly had he gone when Berkeley repented bitterly of having let his enemy slip through his fingers, for some of his advisers told him that Bacon was again meditating armed resistance. At early dawn parties of horsemen galloped up the road to intercept him, boats were sent up the river, the very beds in his lodging house were searched while Lawrence's residence was ransacked from top to bottom.

But Bacon by that time was well on his way to Henrico. When he arrived there his old comrades flocked around him, eager to hear the latest news from Jamestown, and to follow him once more against the Indians. When he told them that the governor had tricked them, that he had no intention of granting a commission and that another costly army was being recruited to cooperate with the "friendly" Indians, "they set their throats in one common key of oaths and curses."

"We will have a commission," they declared, or else we will go down to Jamestown and "pull down the town." And as the news spread from plantation to plantation, angry men came pouring in, promising Bacon that they would follow wherever he led.

They had been rendered desperate by the renewal of the Indian attacks and by the desolate condition of the frontier region. The savages had approached within three miles of Bacon's own residence, he wrote, and had created such terror that many had deserted their houses and plantations, leaving them to the mercy of the enemy. Elizabeth wrote her sister-in-law that since the governor had refused to grant Bacon a commission, "the Indians have had a very good time to do more mischief. They have murdered and destroyed a great many whole families since, and the men resolving not to go under any but your brother, most of the country did rise in arms."

"Thus the raging torrent came down to town." A strange contrast this band presented, as it streamed along through the woods and "old fields" and plantations of Charles City County, to the troop of "loyal gentlemen" whom Berkeley had led over the same road a few weeks before. Side by side were poor planters ground down by excessive taxes; hardy, weatherbeaten frontiersmen; ragged freedmen, some mounted, others trudging along on foot, all united by a common misfortune and by love for their youthful leader. A few talked openly of overthrowing the government, of sharing the property of the rich, of making Lady Berkeley discard her fine clothing for a dress of "canvas linen," but in the main they sought only a redress of grievances and permission to defend themselves from the Indians.

BATTLES ON THE JAMES

Vague rumors which began to filter down to Jamestown that Bacon was on the march were followed by definite news that he was approaching with a force of four hundred foot and one hundred and twenty horse. The village was thrown into a panic. The governor sent out messengers riding posthaste to the adjacent counties for the trained bands to come to his defense. In York a rendezvous was appointed, about one hundred men gathered under four ensigns and a march upon Jamestown actually begun, but many were at heart in sympathy with Bacon and their movements were so slow that they were too late to be of any assistance.

Berkeley himself was all activity. Going out to the narrow neck of land which connected the Jamestown peninsula with the mainland, he began the construction of palisades and the mounting of four great guns which he moved from the fort. But it was too late. The cry arose: "To arms! To arms! Bacon is within two miles of the town." And on all sides it was stated that Bacon had threatened that "if a gun was shot against him he would kill and destroy all." Resistance seemed useless, for there were but thirty soldiers in town and many of them ill affected. So, having ordered the men to lay down their arms and throw the guns from their carriages, Berkeley returned to the State House to await Bacon's arrival.

At two o'clock in the afternoon the little army came streaming across the isthmus at Sandy Bay and down Back Street and formed upon the green in front of the State House. After dispatching parties to take possession of the fort and guard the ferry, Bacon came up to the State House with a double line of fusileers and sent word to the governor that he would like to confer with some members of the Council. Thereupon Colonel Spencer and Colonel Cole came out to ask what he wanted.

Bacon replied that he had come for a commission as General of volunteers against the Indians. And, he added, if it is the purpose of the Assembly to levy taxes on the people to pay for the new army, we will not submit to it.

His men, overhearing what he had said, raised the cry: "No levies! No levies!"

At this juncture Berkeley could restrain himself no longer. Jumping up from his chair in the Council chamber, he rushed out through the porch to the green where Bacon stood at the head of his men. Beside himself with rage and gesticulating wildly, he began upbraiding the young leader, calling him a rebel and traitor and swearing that he would not give him a commission.

Throwing open his coat he cried out: "Here, shoot me, fore God, fair mark, shoot."

But Bacon replied: "No, may it please your honor, we will not hurt a hair of your head, nor of any man's. We are come for a commission to save our lives from the Indians, which you have so often promised and now we will have it before we go."

Thereupon the governor turned and walked to his house a few steps away in the State House block, followed by the members of the Council. But Bacon, in his excitement, came after them, "often tossing his hand from his sword to his hat" and demanding the commission.

In the meanwhile the burgesses had jumped from their seats in the chamber on the second floor of the State House, and rushing to the windows looked down upon the exciting scene below. Regarding this as a sign of indifference to their demand for a commission, Bacon's men cocked their fusils and pointed them up at the windows, at the same time calling out: "We will have it. We will have it."

Bacon added his voice: "You burgesses, we expect your speedy result."

One of the members, who was known to many of Bacon's men, waved a handkerchief out of the window, saying: "For God's sake hold your hands; forbear a little and you shall have what you please."

An hour or so later Bacon came into the Long Room to make a personal appeal to the burgesses for a commission. When the speaker sat mute, Thomas Blayton of Charles City County rose and explained that the governor alone, as the vice-regent of the King, and not the Assembly, had the right to issue commissions.

When Blayton sat down Bacon addressed the burgesses at some length, explaining the urgent need for an investigation into the handling of public revenues, deploring the high taxes, pleading for a redress of grievances and reiterating that he had taken up arms only to protect the colony from the Indians. When he had finished, the frightened burgesses sat in silence, so that in a moment he turned with a frown and left the room. However, he had no sooner gone than the burgesses, many of them in sympathy with him, others overawed, sent a message to the governor advising him to grant the commission. Urged also by his Council, Berkeley finally yielded, and a commission to Bacon was duly drawn up and signed.

But Bacon was not satisfied. The next morning he entered the Assembly Hall with an armed guard and demanded that the governor's most notorious henchmen be debarred from holding any office, that Berkeley's letter to the King declaring him a rebel and traitor be publicly contradicted and that Captain Gardiner of the *Adam and Eve* be forced to pay him £70 for his sloop which was lost at the time of his capture.

When these demands came before Berkeley he swore that he would suffer death rather than submit to them. But the burgesses urged him to grant whatever was required, for the frontiersmen were making dire threats and it was feared Bacon could not restrain them. So a letter was written to the King and signed by the governor, the Council and the burgesses, justifying Bacon's conduct and testifying to his loyalty. Blank commissions for officers to serve under Bacon were presented for signature and several of Berkeley's friends were committed to prison. The governor was persuaded to grant everything required of him so long as it did not concern "life and limb," in order to get rid of the rebels.

In June 1776 Thomas Jefferson penned the world famous Declaration of Independence, proclaiming that men are endowed by nature with certain inalienable rights, that governments are instituted to preserve these rights, that governments derive their power from the consent of the governed, that the people may alter the government if it is false to the ends for which it was established. At the time he seems to have been totally unaware that his fellow Virginians a century earlier almost to a day, had acted upon these very principles under the leadership of Nathaniel Bacon. So greatly had time and the misrepresentations of his enemies obscured the real Bacon that not until 1804, when Rufus King sent him an old chronicle of the uprising, did Jefferson begin to realize Bacon's patriotic motives. Even then he did not recognize him as a martyr to American rights and his movement as the forerunner of the American Revolution.

Certainly in 1810, when W. W. Hening's *Virginia Statutes at Large*, including the so-called Bacon's laws, was first published, Jefferson must have gained a clearer understanding of the greatest popular uprising of the colonial period, in which it is more than probable that his own great-grandfather played an inconspicuous part. Many of the burgesses who met in the Long Room of the State House on June 6, 1676, had been elected by the reform party at a time when the people were disgusted with the governor and bitterly hostile to the old corrupt régime. How much they could have accomplished had not Bacon taken command of the situation can only be conjectured. Already they had permitted reform to be pushed aside for Indian affairs, and even in Indian affairs the governor was still threatening and commanding and carrying things with a high hand as of old.

But with Bacon's men in possession of Jamestown, the governor a virtual prisoner and Bacon himself dominating the Assembly, one liberal law after another was put upon the statute books. Of first importance was the repeal of a law of 1670 which restricted the right to vote to men owning a freehold or a residence, and the passage of a new statute specifically extending the franchise to all freemen.

The burgesses thus served notice on the King and his governor that they could not accept the principle that because a man owned no property he had no interest in the government and no right to a voice in shaping its policies.

Then followed a series of acts sweeping away many of the abuses of which the people had long complained. Councillors were no longer to be exempt from taxation; the secretary of the colony, all clerks of courts, sheriffs, surveyors, collectors and other officers were forbidden to charge more for their services than the sums prescribed by law; the voters in each county were to select representatives to sit with the justices of the peace in assessing the county taxes; vestries were no longer to be self-perpetuating but were to be chosen every three years by the voters of the parish; no person was to be sheriff "for more than one year successively," the office devolving on the justices in rotation; no two of the offices of sheriff, clerk of the court, surveyor and escheator could be held by any one man simultaneously; no member of the Council could sit with the justices of the peace.

When these bills were brought to Berkeley for his signature, he must have choked with rage, for they struck a telling blow at the whole system of privilege and corruption on which he had built up his power. Nonetheless, he was induced to sign, knowing that he could declare illegal the entire proceedings of the Assembly as soon as Bacon had withdrawn his men.

And the time for Bacon to leave was now at hand.

On June 25 a messenger came riding into town with the news that the Indians had made another raid on the frontier and had murdered eight persons on the upper Chickahominy, not more than forty miles from Jamestown. This created great alarm among Bacon's men as many lived in this section and preparations were made for a hasty leave.

That evening at sunset Bacon approached a group of burgesses who were bidding each other goodbye before setting out for their homes. "Which of you gentlemen shall I entreat to write a few words for me?" he asked, unfolding a handful of papers.

Lawrence, who was at his elbow, pointed to Thomas Mathews, saying: "That gentleman writes very well."

So Mathews, despite his fear that it might bring down on him the governor's anger, was forced to sit up all night filling in the blank commissions signed by Berkeley and adding such names and other matters as Bacon dictated. With the break of dawn the drums beat, the infantry fell into line, the horsemen mounted and the army moved out past Sandy Bay and headed for the frontier.

Now once more all Virginia was filled with martial preparations. Some of the leading men in the colony, many of them officers in the trained bands, were induced to accept Bacon's commissions, not realizing that they might be illegal despite Berkeley's forced signature. Companies of men were formed and marched off to the frontiers; arms, ammunition and stores of all kinds were placed on sloops and sent up the rivers; friendly Indians were pressed into service; horsemen went clattering over the dirt roads. Bacon himself rode from county to county at the head of a troop of cavalry to superintend the operations.

Even though the people were in sympathy with Bacon and wished to support him in his war with the Indians, many a planter was angered when a party of rough frontiersmen rode up to his house and took away one or two of his horses, his fusil, and part of his store of bacon and corn—and cursed him roundly if he protested. Some of Sir William's friends put up a show of resistance, but they were intimidated or overpowered. Mathew Gale, one of Bacon's officers, threatened Colonel Mathew Kemp, of the Gloucester cavalry, "with all the execrable oaths he could imagine, he would pistol him." Against John Mann, Gale burst out in "many fearful oaths, as God damn his blood, sink him and rot him, he would ruin him," and threatened to send for General Bacon to bring a hundred horse to overrun and ruin all Gloucester.

Bacon himself ordered the arrest of Major Lawrence Smith and Major Thomas Hawkins, whom he found actively engaged in raising armed forces. These men had both done good service in protecting the upper Rappahannock region from the Indians and claimed now that they had no hostile intentions against Bacon. But the young commander insisted that the war should be carried on entirely under his personal direction as commander of all the forces of the colony, and he feared that Smith and Hawkins might place their troops at the governor's disposal.

By the end of July when Bacon's preparations were completed, he appointed the falls of the James as the place of rendezvous and set out to take command of his troops. Here he drew up his army of seven hundred horse and six hundred foot, all well armed and provisioned for two months, to make a brief address. He assured them of his loyalty to the King.

It was true, he said, that he had secured his commission by force, but he had been actuated only by a desire to serve his Prince and his country, urged on by the "cries of his brethrens' blood that alarmed him and wakened him to this public revenge." Then, when he had finished, he took the oath of allegiance and supremacy himself and urged his soldiers to do likewise. After this he required them all to take an oath of fidelity to him as their general, that they would report to him any plot against his person or against his followers, that they would have no dealings with the so-called friendly Indians, that they would give no information concerning his actions or the movements of the army, that they would report any news of the plans and plotting of the Indians.

Night had fallen on the camp beside the James, all was in readiness for the expedition and orders had been issued to march the next day, when a message reached Bacon which threw all into confusion. For some time after Bacon's departure from Jamestown, Berkeley had remained passive, without revoking his commission or again proclaiming him a rebel. Not that he hesitated to begin a civil war by summoning the militia and attacking Bacon's army in the rear, but he had good reason to believe that the soldiers would not follow him. So when he received an address, supposedly from the people of Gloucester but in reality drawn up by a few of his own friends, complaining that Bacon had stripped the county of arms and asking the governor to protect them, he instantly sprang into action.

"This petition is most willingly granted," he wrote exultantly. "And I further declare that I am bound to grant it, for the allegiance I owe to his Majesty and the care he hath imposed on me to preserve his loyal subjects from all outrages and oppressions, to which they have been lately too much submitted by the tyranny and usurpation of Nathaniel Bacon, junior, who never had any commission from me but that which with arms he extracted from the Assembly, which in effect is no more than if a thief should take my purse and make me own I gave it him freely. So in effect his commission whatever it is, is void in law and nature."

So mounting his horse he rode over to Gloucester, and sending out a call for the trained bands, made preparations to regain his lost authority by force of arms. But when the men had assembled and learned that they were expected "to fight against their countrymen, neighbors and friends," they stood for a moment irresolute. Then a low murmur began throughout the ranks: "Bacon! Bacon! Bacon!" and turning their backs on the governor, they walked away still muttering: "Bacon! Bacon! Bacon!"

Crushed by this evidence of the people's affection for his youthful rival and wearied by his excessive exertions, the governor "fainted away on horseback in the field."

Had Bacon realized how futile Berkeley's efforts would prove, he would not have permitted them to divert him from his campaign against the Indians. But he dared not march off into the forests with the prospect of having Sir William coming up on his rear. So "immediately he causes the drums to beat and the trumpet to sound for calling his men together." When they were lined up before him, he delivered a brief address:

Gentlemen and fellow soldiers: The news just now brought me may not a little startle you as well as myself. But seeing it is not altogether unexpected, we may the better bear it and provide our remedies. The governor is now in Gloucester County trying to raise forces against us, having declared us rebels and traitors, if true, crimes indeed too great for pardon. Our clear consciences herein are our best witnesses, whereas their own guilty consciences will deprive them of the courage to face us. It is revenge that hurries them on without regard to the people's safety, for they would rather we should be murdered and our ghosts sent after those of our slaughtered countrymen, than for us to live to disturb their trade with the Indians. Now then we must be forced to turn our swords to our own defense or expose ourselves to their mercy as we seek our fortune in the woods while the country lies in blood and wasting like a candle at both ends.

How can we proceed with enemies in arms behind us to cut off our provisions and supplies, and seize those who are returning because of wounds or sickness? So, sound at heart, while we are unwearied and at our full strength, let us descend upon them to find out why they have taken arms against us, why they should seek to destroy those they have raised for their defense to preserve them against the fury of the heathen, why they seek our lives who are trying to preserve theirs. We call all the ages to witness that never before was such treachery heard of, such wickedness and inhumanity. But they are damned cowards and you shall see that they will not dare to meet us in the field to try the justice of our cause.

Whereupon the soldiers raised a shout of approval. "Amen! Amen!" they cried, "we are all ready! We would rather die in the field than be hanged like rogues or slaughtered by the savages." So the order to march was given and the army streamed away through Henrico and New Kent and descended on Gloucester. But Sir William, deserted by all save a few loyal gentlemen, had fled for safety to the Eastern Shore. Here, protected from his triumphant rival by the waters of the broad Chesapeake Bay, he rallied around him what forces he could, laid his plans for future operations, and wrote to the English government his denunciations of Bacon and his excuses for himself.

When Bacon found himself master of all Virginia from the Potomac to Lower Norfolk and from the Chesapeake to the frontier, he realized fully that he had assumed an important and dangerous responsibility. He had become, unexpectedly and against his own wishes, the Cromwell of the colony. He must preserve order, see that the regular functions of the government were not disturbed, keep open the courts and perhaps summon the Assembly. If he could have laid his hands on Berkeley he would have kept him under guard until his own and his followers' case had been put before the King. He would have told of the Indian massacres, of Sir William's refusal to consent to an expedition to end them, of the poverty of the people and the injustices to which they had been subjected, and finally would have prayed for pardon for seeking redress in arms. But since the governor was out of his reach and since he had at hand no means for communicating with England, he had to content himself with assuming control of civil as well as military affairs and postponing to a later date his explanations and excuses.

His first step was to lead the army to the hamlet of Middle Plantation, where he pitched camp, probably near the present Palace Green, in the heart of Williamsburg. He then sent out squadrons of horse through various parts of the colony to scatter any bands which might be gathering under Berkeley's orders and to arrest as many of his leading supporters as he could lay his hands on—Colonel Richard Lee, Philip Lightfoot and many others. Those who pledged themselves "to return home and live quietly," Bacon set at liberty, but others were taken to Middle Plantation and kept in confinement. Richard Lee was imprisoned for seven weeks, "whereby he received great prejudice to his health by hard usage." All accounts agree, however, even those by Bacon's bitterest enemies, that he was not inclined to be harsh or cruel. But he was engaged in very serious business, indeed, he knew that his own life was in peril, and he could not afford to tolerate insubordination or treachery. It was but natural, then, that when he discovered a spy in his camp, he should have had him tried by court martial and sentenced to death. As the culprit was led out before the army drawn up to witness the hanging, Bacon called out that if any man "would speak a word to save him he should not suffer." When there was universal silence, the execution was carried through.

To Bacon's headquarters at Middle Plantation came his ardent friends Richard Lawrence and William Drummond, to advise him in the all-important matter of taking over the government. If we may believe Thomas Mathews who knew him well, Lawrence was the original instigator of the uprising. He himself had heard Lawrence discuss the possibility of rectifying the abuses in the government resulting from the avarice and French despotic methods of the governor, he said. Likewise he knew him to have been a thinking man, honest, affable, without blemish and most persuasive in conversation. Living at Jamestown, to which people resorted from all parts of Virginia, he found opportunity to "instil his notions" in men's minds. As for Drummond, he was a Scotsman who had formerly been governor of North Carolina, and was known as a sober gentleman of good repute, honest and able.

With this experienced and devoted pair at his elbow, Bacon now issued a manifesto justifying his own conduct and accusing Berkeley of tyranny, injustice and cruelty. As for himself, he confessed that he was guilty of treason if treason consisted of pleading the cause of the oppressed, of aiming at the public good, of saving the colony from the savages. But he said:

We cannot find one single spot of rebellion in our hearts, for we have not tried to overthrow the government, have harmed no man and have refrained from riot and plunder. But we are all witnesses of the corruption of the government, how men of poor extraction and mean estates have been lifted to posts of importance, how these men have sucked up the public treasury like sponges, how they have discouraged trade, the liberal arts and science. We are accused of turning our arms against the so-called friendly Indians, but we have proof that they have for years been our enemies, robbing us and attacking us. It is the fault of the governor who supplied them with arms and ammunition that our "plantations are deserted, the blood of our dear brethren spilt," and "murder upon murder renewed upon us." Yet we abhor the name of rebel and do "unanimously desire to represent our sad and heavy grievances to his most sacred Majesty as our refuge and sanctuary."

Realizing that resistance to his authority would come almost entirely from the upper class, Bacon now made an effort to bind them to him by involving them in his plans. So he sent out a summons to some of the leading men in the colony—councillors, burgesses, officers in the militia, sheriffs—to meet at Middle Plantation to confer with him upon the Indian war and the preservation of law and order. This placed these gentlemen in a quandary. Should they ignore the summons and flee to Sir William, Bacon might denounce them as enemies of the people and confiscate their estates; if they took part in his conference, the governor might proclaim them rebels.

In the end no less than seventy men, including such leading planters as John Page, Thomas Ballard, Philip Lightfoot and Thomas Milner, gathered on August 3, at the residence of Captain Otho Thorpe and waited for Bacon to lay his plans before them.

A dramatic scene it was—the group of leading planters, some travel-stained from hard riding, their serious faces betraying their anxiety, huddled together in the great hall; Lawrence and Drummond conferring with the clerk of the Assembly over the drawing up of protests and oaths; the young leader of twenty-nine who had wrested the government from the King's governor and was preparing to resist the King himself. Even now perhaps Bacon did not realize that he was striking out against two separate though closely associated forces—the authority of the English government in the colony and the vested power of the local aristocracy represented in part by the very men who faced him. He could reiterate his loyalty, could point to the Indian murders as the sole cause of his taking up arms, but the logical course of events was forcing him into the same position taken by the American patriots a century later who declared their independence because they found that they could not have liberty without it.

But for the present he stressed the Indian war. Addressing the assembled gentlemen, he asked their advice as to how the country should be protected from the governor's attacks so that he could go out against the savages. He could not ask his men to risk their lives in the woods for the common good and then bring them back to have their throats cut. Would it not be proper, he asked, to draw up a test or oath to be subscribed by the whole country not to aid Sir William against his army? This met with a murmur of assent and the clerk was ordered to put the oath into form.

But when Bacon next proposed that all swear to resist any royal forces sent to Virginia until the King could be properly informed as to the origin of the trouble, there was bitter opposition. Why, this was treason. They would all hang for resisting the troops. Bacon argued that it was a necessary part of the oath, without which there could be no peace, no security for himself, for the army and the country. If they would not give him this measure of protection he was resolved to surrender his commission to the Assembly and let the country find some other person to risk his life against the Indians.

In the midst of this heated discussion a gunner came in from the fort at Tindal's Point on the York River, imploring aid against the Indians. Scores of poor people who had taken refuge there would be defenseless, he said, unless munitions and arms were rushed to them. Why, how was this possible, Bacon asked. How could the strongest fortress in Virginia be in danger of surprise? The gunner told him that the day before Sir William had come over from the Eastern Shore and after conveying all the guns and ammunition on board his vessel had sailed away. This news produced a sensation at the gathering, for it seemed to substantiate Bacon's charge that the old governor would willingly sacrifice the people to his own stubbornness and vanity. One after another the assembled gentlemen affixed their signatures to the oath, said goodbye to Bacon and turned homeward.

As they rode along through the peaceful plantations with their fields of tobacco plants, or ferried over the broad rivers, there came to some of them a disturbing vision, a vision of British warships in the James and the York, of regiments of redcoats on Virginia soil, of an enraged old governor and of bodies dangling on the scaffold.

It came also to a frightened woman in Henrico who fervently wished her husband and herself back in Friston Hall in far-off Suffolk.

And at Friston Hall it came to a sorrowing old man who prayed King Charles to pardon his only son for having permitted his neighbors to persuade him to lead them out against the savages in defiance of the governor's orders.

It came again and again to young Bacon himself as he was drawn along by the sequence of events. One day Thomas Mathews in a conversation with Drummond warned him to be wary as the governor had marked him for revenge. "Mr. Mathews," replied the Scotsman, "I am in over shoes, I had as well be in over boots." Bacon himself might have given the same reply. Avowing at first that he was acting only for self-preservation against the Indians, he was led on to gaining his commission by force of arms, then to making war on the governor, then to establishing a government of his own, then to planning resistance to the English troops and finally to plotting for independence in conjunction with other colonies.

It was early in September that Bacon had an interesting and illuminating conversation with a certain John Goode, a fellow citizen of Henrico.

"There is a report that Sir William Berkeley has sent to the King for two thousand redcoats, and I do believe it may be true," said Bacon. "Tell me your opinion, may not five hundred Virginians beat them, we having the same advantages against them the Indians have against us?"

"On the contrary I think five hundred redcoats may either subject or ruin Virginia," Goode replied.

Bacon had no way of foreseeing that eight decades later an English army would march through the American woods to a terrible defeat at the hands of the French and Indians, but he now showed that he understood exactly the conditions which brought about Braddock's downfall.

"You talk strangely," he said. "Are we not acquainted with the country, so that we can lay ambuscades? Can we not hide behind trees to render their discipline of no avail? Are we not as good or better shots than they?"

But now Goode pointed out how defenseless Virginia was against any power having control of the water, because of the four great rivers which ran up into the heart of the country. It was a fatal weakness, a weakness which was to be only too clearly demonstrated during the Revolution, the War of 1812 and the Civil War.

"They can accomplish what I have said without hazard or coming into such disadvantages," he replied, "by taking opportunities of landing where there is no opposition, firing our houses and fences, destroying our cattle, preventing trade and cutting off imports."

"We can prevent their making any progress in such mischiefs. Moreover, since the climate will not agree with them, they will be worn down by sickness."

Here Goode switched to another discouraging aspect of the situation. "You see, sir, that in a manner all the principal men in the country, who dislike your proceedings, will, you may be sure, make common cause with the redcoats."

"I will see to it that they do not have the opportunity."

"Sir, you speak as though you designed a total defection from the King and our native country."

At this Bacon smiled: "Why, have not many princes lost their dominions so?"

"They have been such peoples as have been able to subsist without their princes," Goode pointed out. "The poverty of Virginia is such that the major part of the inhabitants can scarce shift one year without supplies from England. You may be sure that the people who so fondly follow you, when they come to feel the miserable want of food and clothing, will be in great haste to leave you. Besides there are many people in Virginia who receive considerable benefits from parents and friends in England and many who expect patrimonies and inheritances which they will not want to lose."

"I know of nothing with which this country could not in time supply itself save ammunition and iron," said Bacon, "and I believe the King of France or the States of Holland would be glad to trade with us."

"Sir, our King is a very great prince and his amity is infinitely more valuable to these countries than any advantage they could reap from Virginia. They will not provoke his displeasure by supporting the rebels here.

Besides, your followers do not think themselves engaged against the King's authority, but merely against the Indians."

"But I think otherwise, and I am confident that it is the mind of this colony and of Maryland as well as Carolina, to cast off their governors. And if we cannot prevail by arms to make our conditions of peace, or obtain the privilege to elect our own governor, we may retire to the Roanoke and establish our own government there."

"Sir, the prosecuting of this design will produce utter ruin and distraction," Goode replied, "and I hope you will excuse me from having any part in it."

"I am glad to know your mind, but I think this proceeds from mere cowardice." Then, after a pause, he asked: "What should a gentleman do in my situation? You as good as tell me I must flee or hang."

"I should advise an humble submission to the Assembly which gave you your commission and an acknowledgement of your errors."

With this Goode left him to meditate alone upon his problems, his future plans, his hopes and fears for the colony and for himself.

It would have been well had the English government printed this extraordinary conversation, which was reported to them just as it took place, and required each officer in any way concerned with colonial affairs to read it. Had Grenville known of it and had he grasped its lessons, there might never have been an American Revolution. It might have startled George III and Lord North to know that in the seventeenth century a popular leader in Virginia had risen in arms, had made himself master of the province, and had contemplated a union of the colonies for the purpose of winning autonomy if not complete independence.

Bacon's plans came to nothing, not only because of his untimely death, but because they were premature. As Goode pointed out, Virginia was almost defenseless against either a naval attack or an economic blockade. Food she had in abundance, but England had only to cut off the flow of manufactured goods to bring acute distress to the planters. A century later, when the settlements had pushed westward past deep water beyond the reach of either warships or merchant vessels, when many families had begun to make their own clothes and other needed articles, the old sense of dependence had faded. Moreover, in 1775 a kinship had developed between the various colonies, born in part of the French and Indian war, totally lacking a century before, when Boston seemed as remote to the Virginia planters as Paris or Rome. But the forces which made for independence in the time of Washington and John Adams were in active operation at the time of Nathaniel Bacon. The rising in Virginia might be suppressed, Bacon might be denounced as a rebel, and his chief supporters led to the gallows, but in the end these forces would be too strong even for England itself to withstand.

CHAPTER V
PROLOGUE TO THE AMERICAN REVOLUTION

"DEATH WHY SO CRUEL?"

Prologue to the American Revolution

BERKELEY FOUND THE EASTERN SHORE NOT ONLY A HAVEN of refuge but an excellent base for operations against Bacon's forces. When he landed, accompanied only by Philip Ludwell and four other faithful followers, he made his headquarters at "Arlington," the plantation of Colonel John Custis, on Old Plantation Creek, in Northampton County. This place, which was provided with an ample harbor, was admirably suited as a base for swift raids on the shores of southeast Virginia, for it was within twenty-five miles of the mouths of the Rappahannock, the York and the James. Moreover, it was close to the entrance to Chesapeake Bay, and thus convenient for intercepting merchant vessels coming in from England and enlisting them in the governor's cause. To "Arlington" Berkeley summoned all "loyal" men to meet him, on pain of being denounced as rebels.

Many a leading planter of the Western Shore, leaving his estate to Bacon's mercy, loaded his plate and other valuables on the plantation sloop and sailed across the bay to place himself under Berkeley's standard. Soon the halls and outhouses of "Arlington" were crowded with the "great men" of Virginia—Colonel William Cole, Colonel Joseph Bridger, Ralph Wormeley, Major Robert Beverley, Captain William Digges and many others. With them came henchmen, relatives and indentured workers, so that the whole made a force of considerable size. Berkeley appointed Custis major general and gave him the command of all the loyal forces, summoned the trained bands of Northampton and Accomac, set guards at every harbor and navigable creek, and gathered stores of arms and ammunition in preparation for raids on the Western Shore and to repel a possible invasion by Bacon's men.

The small planters of Accomac and Northampton had preferred to stay out of the civil war. They had escaped the Indian raids because of their geographic situation, and so were not fired with resentment at Berkeley's remissness in protecting the colony. They had no desire to risk their necks for young Bacon whom they had never seen and whose intentions had been misrepresented to them. On the other hand, they had little enthusiasm for Berkeley, whose oppressions were as well known on the Eastern Shore as elsewhere. But since they had either to obey his summons or defy his authority, most of the militiamen gathered at the muster fields with their arms, ready to follow the bidding of their regular officers.

Amid the startlingly rapid series of events of that fateful summer, both Berkeley and Bacon seem for the moment to have overlooked the overwhelming importance of naval supremacy upon the outcome of the struggle. The great Chesapeake Bay, together with the James, the York, the Rappahannock and the Potomac, were the natural highways of the region. The side which controlled them could advance with impunity into the heart of the country, could land forces at unexpected points, cut off isolated garrisons, force the enemy in their marches to go many miles out of their way to round the heads of navigation, cut off communication with England, and command the cargoes of incoming merchant vessels. If Berkeley could gain control of the bay he was almost as safe from Bacon's men as he would have been in England; if Bacon controlled it he could attack the governor at pleasure with the full force at his command.

Bacon was the first to grasp this situation. Since England was at peace and there had been no fear of foreign invasion there were no warships in Virginia waters. Moreover, it was midsummer, too early for the arrival of the tobacco ships from England with their cargoes of manufactured goods. But there were several vessels in the James River, among them the *Rebecca* commanded by Captain Larimore and a smaller vessel under Captain John Moore. Placing three hundred men under the command of Giles Bland and Captain William Carver, "a very good seaman" and "a stout resolute fellow," he ordered them to capture these ships as a nucleus for a navy. The English shipmasters knew nothing of the grievances of the people of the colony, they looked upon Bacon and his men as rebels and so resented any attempt to divert them from their regular traffic to the dangerous business of fighting the King's governor and possibly the royal frigates. So when Bacon's men came swarming around them, probably in rowboats and sloops, Larimore fired on them.

His resistance was in vain, both ships were taken, and Larimore himself was imprisoned.

Carver and Bland next planned to take a merchant vessel commanded by Christopher Eveling, which seems to have been moored further down the James. It was suspected that Eveling was harboring Berkeley and some of his chief henchmen, for when Bacon sent several soldiers with search warrants he refused to permit them to come on board, denouncing him as a rebel and terming him "Oliver" Bacon. So preparations were set on foot to equip the *Rebecca* for an attack on his ship, by drawing her up at Jamestown and mounting on board several of the great guns from the brick fort. Unfortunately, Eveling got word of what was going on, and, hoisting sail, headed down the river and out through the Capes for England.

This proved to be a real disaster, for Eveling took with him letters from Berkeley, Ludwell and others, misrepresenting Bacon's cause and denouncing him as a traitor. Thus the governor would gain the ear of the King and Privy Council before the people of Virginia and their young leader could make known their grievances and their motives in taking arms. When Charles learned that his governor had fled from his capital and that all Virginia except two counties was in the hands of the insurgents, he would almost certainly send over troops and warships to reestablish the royal authority.

Had Bacon captured Eveling's ship, and, after confiscating the letters of his enemies sent it to England under guard with his own dispatches, telling of Berkeley's oppressions, the sufferings of the people, the terrible Indian raids, the governor's refusal to permit them to protect themselves and disavowing any treasonable intent, the future might have been very different. Charles II could hardly have condoned Bacon's conduct, but probably he would have tried conciliation rather than force. As it was, from the moment Eveling got away, Bacon realized that eventually he would have to face not only Berkeley but the armed naval and military forces of England.

Despite this disappointment, Carver and Bland, having put all in readiness, sailed down the river with the *Rebecca*, now a formidable war vessel with her sixteen guns, a small bark carrying four guns and a sloop. On board were two hundred and fifty armed men, together with the English sailors and Captain Larimore, whose knowledge of his vessel and of Virginia waters made his presence indispensable. Arriving at the mouth of the James they encountered an incoming vessel of ninety tons and added her to the little fleet. Then they stationed themselves near Cape Charles to intercept other merchant ships from England as they came in one by one. In this way they hoped to build up a navy strong enough not only to keep Berkeley bottled up on the Eastern Shore but to resist the British frigates which they feared would be sent against them.

So now Bacon, with his land forces in control of all Virginia save Accomac and Northampton, with his little navy guarding the Virginia waters and likely to grow stronger and stronger, thought the time had come to carry out his long delayed expedition against the Indians.

Once more the army broke camp and headed for Henrico, with the intention of making a second expedition against the remnants of the Susquehannocks and Occaneechees. But after arriving at the falls of the James, information came to Bacon which made him alter his plans.

The Indians were on the warpath again, this time not on the frontier, but in the very heart of Gloucester, one of the older counties. Families which had thought themselves safe from the Indian terror had been aroused by the warwhoop, to be cut down or dragged away to the woods for a lingering death. Seven were killed within four miles of Tindal's Point, across the York River from the present Yorktown, and eight near the county courthouse. The savages slowly roasted their wretched captives alive, cutting off pieces of flesh and offering it to other victims to eat, pulling off their finger and toe nails, slitting them open and running their intestines around the trunks of trees.

This put an entirely new light upon the situation. The frontiersmen had long contended that the so-called friendly Indians, to whom Berkeley had looked for the protection of the exposed plantations, had taken part in some of the blood-thirsty raids. It was not possible to identify individuals or tribes even when terrified fugitives peered at them from their hiding places, because war paint served to disguise them. But it was known that war parties had come from the direction of the Indian towns, where, it was thought, they must have found food and protection, if not recruits for their incursions.

The recent murders in Gloucester not only confirmed this belief, but pointed directly at Berkeley's friends the Pamunkeys. It will be remembered that this tribe had fled from their town on the Pamunkey River in the present King William County, over the Mattapony, to take refuge in the Dragon Swamp. They had there a hiding place that was very difficult to find, easy of defense and admirably suited for a base of operations on the plantations between the York and the Rappahannock. The swamp ran for many miles along both banks of the upper waters of the Piankitanck River, through a heavily wooded and almost uninhabited country, but within a few miles of the tobacco fields of Middlesex and Gloucester, thus affording a hidden pathway into the heart of those counties. The savages who perpetrated the murders in eastern Gloucester must have approached down the Dragon Swamp, and this would have been almost impossible without the knowledge and perhaps the aid of the Pamunkeys.

So with this threat in his rear and the treachery of the Pamunkeys exposed, Bacon gave up his original plans and directed his march eastward. At the same time another force recruited from the northern counties and commanded by Colonel Giles Brent, himself half Indian, the son of a Maryland gentleman and the "empress" of the Piscataways, was set in motion to join him. The junction of the two forces was effected on the headwaters of the York and the search began. But they were now in a region where their movements were impeded by swamps and rivers made almost impassable by continued rains. When the supply of provisions began to run low because of the prolonged delay, Bacon drew up his men and delivered one of those inspiring addresses of which he was master.

He feared the badness of the weather would not only delay their march, he said, but might so reduce their stores of food as to cause serious privation. Therefore, he would at once put them all upon restricted rations. But they were very close to the outlying plantations and if any so desired they were at liberty to return. Those whose courage was great and whose resolution to avenge the blood of their friends was stronger than their regard for their stomachs, he hoped would remain with him. As for the weak of heart and cowardly, he would rather have them go than remain to eat the food needed for the resolute and brave.

When he had concluded only three men stepped forth. So when these had been disarmed and sent back amid the jeers of the army, Bacon gave the order to march. Throwing out ten Indian scouts to prevent surprise and discover the way, he proceeded along a trail through the woods. Suddenly the scouts came upon a small Indian village upon a point of dry land with marsh ground to right and left, and a skirmish ensued. As the reports of the fusils came to them through the woods the English rushed to the attack. But the marsh proved an effective barrier, and while they were floundering in the mire, the savages made good their escape. So, all that was accomplished was the "taking of a little Indian child and the killing of an Indian woman."

Again the discouraging task of searching for the main body of the Pamunkeys through the woods and along the marshy bottom of Dragon Run was taken up. The Queen of the Pamunkeys, learning through her scouts that Bacon was on her track, fled in haste, leaving behind her stores of corn and "all her goods."

As the English marched on, following narrow forest paths which seemed to lead nowhere, they came upon an old Indian woman, the nurse of the Queen, and demanded that she guide them to the Pamunkey hiding place. Pretending to obey, the squaw set out through the woods, the English in a long line trailing behind. After a day and a half it dawned on them that they were going in exactly the wrong direction. So they knocked the old woman on the head and retraced their steps to the swamp. This time they were more fortunate, and emerging upon an opening, found "several nations of Indians" encamped in close proximity to each other. Without hesitation the English charged in among the huts, while the savages, taken by surprise, put up no resistance but fled into the woods and swamps with the loss of five or six men and women.

The expedition had now lasted far longer than had been anticipated, provisions were very low, many of the men were exhausted from constant marching and were impatient at their lack of success. Yet Bacon was unwilling to return until he had struck a telling blow against the Indians. His immediate followers, many of them veterans of the Occaneechee expedition, were still determined to go on, but the northern troops, "tired, murmuring, impatient, half-starved," demanded permission to return home. When they had marched off, Bacon with but four hundred men moved on "beating the swamps up and down," until "almost all his provisions were spent." In this crisis he drew his men up to address them. A dramatic moment it was as the determined young leader faced his little army of tired, hungry, ragged men, in the depths of the Virginia forest.

"Gentlemen, the indefatigable pains we have taken deserve better success than we have met with. But there is nothing that cannot be accomplished by labor and industry, which makes me hope we may yet meet the heathen to square accounts for their barbarous cruelties done us. I should rather my body should lie rotting in the woods and never again see an Englishman's face, than fail in this service which the country expects of me and I vowed to perform against these heathen. Should I return without having punished and intimidated them, they would be as much animated as the English discouraged. My enemies would seize the opportunity to insult me and misrepresent me, saying that my defense of the country is a mere pretense to cloak other designs. But that all may see how devoted I am to our cause, I am determined to go on with any who will follow me, even though we have to undergo the worst hardships of this wilderness, if need be subsisting on nuts and horseflesh. Therefore I shall set my standard outside the camp, so that those who wish to remain can rally around it. The rest have free leave to return to their homes."

The next morning, as the sun broke through the trees upon the camp, the little army divided itself into two parts, the one setting out on their return journey to the plantations, the other, numbering probably not more than one hundred and fifty men, continuing in their pursuit of the Indians.

This time success crowned their efforts. They had gone but a few miles when they came upon the main Pamunkey settlement. Bacon's men saw before them a bit of high ground, protected in front and on two sides by swamps, and covered with "thickets, small oaks, saplings, chinquapin bushes and grape vines," behind them the lurking savages. Overjoyed at finding their elusive enemy, they charged, probably from the one side not protected by the marshes, and swept all before them. As the terrified Indians fled, the English followed close upon their heels killing many and capturing others who found escape cut off by the surrounding marshes. When at last the trumpet sounded to summon the men from the pursuit, no less than forty-five prisoners were brought in and delivered to Bacon, together with stores of various kinds—mats, baskets, matchcoats, parcels of wampum, skins, furs, pieces of linen, broadcloth and other English goods. A great triumph it was, and a fitting ending to the long days of hunger and of marching.

The Queen of the Pamunkeys, fleeing at the first approach of the English, escaped into the woods accompanied only by an Indian boy of ten years. At last she determined to return to throw herself upon Bacon's mercy, but, stumbling upon a dead Indian woman lying athwart her path, she was so terrified that she hastened back into the wilderness. Here she wandered exhausted and famished, preserving life only by "gnawing sometimes upon the leg of a terrapin which the little boy found in the woods."

When Bacon's triumphant little band emerged from the woods in what is now King and Queen County, they were greeted with the terrible news that during their absence Berkeley had captured Bland and Carver's little fleet, had reoccupied Jamestown and was ready in overwhelming force to dispute with them the supremacy of Virginia. This disastrous situation could be laid chiefly to Captain Larimore's hostility to Bacon and his desire to recover his ship. While the vessels under Carver and Bland were cruising off Cape Charles, Larimore managed to get a message on shore to Berkeley, promising that he and the English sailors would lend their assistance if he would send out a force to capture his ship.

Berkeley hesitated, for he had assumed that Larimore was serving willingly under Bacon and not by compulsion. It might be a trap to ensnare some of his men and prepare the way for an invasion of the Eastern Shore. On the other hand, his situation was desperate. In a few weeks Bacon would be returning from his Pamunkey expedition, and then he would certainly put his army aboard a fleet of sloops and under the protection of Bland and Carver's guns sail across the bay to invade Northampton. Earnest and prolonged were the consultations over the tableboard at "Arlington," but in the end Berkeley was persuaded to accept Larimore's offer, however desperate the attempt to take the fleet might be.

Thereupon the governor concealed two small boats, manned by twenty-six men under the command of Philip Ludwell, in a creek ready for instant action. He then sent word to Captain Carver that he would like to treat with him, presumably about a peaceful settlement of his differences with Bacon. Carver no doubt thought this a good opportunity to have the stigma of rebellion lifted from himself and his associates, but he told Berkeley he dared not trust his promise that he would permit him to return to the fleet in safety. Thereupon Berkeley gave him the assurance in writing, "under his hand and seal." Upon this Carver put his head into the fatal noose, by sailing ashore in the sloop and entering into a long conference with the governor. Berkeley apparently knew Carver's weakness. As they talked over possible plans of reconciliation, he kept plying the Captain with liquor until he was half-drunk and oblivious to the fact that he had stayed far too long.

While this scene was being enacted on shore, stirring events were occurring a short distance away in the bay. Larimore and his men, who now were equal in numbers to the Virginians, managed to lock the doors of the gun room of the ship, where most of the arms were stored. Then he stood up on the poop deck and "flirted a handkerchief about his nose," as a signal to watchers on shore that all was in readiness. Thereupon Ludwell's two boats emerged from hiding and headed for the fleet. As they approached, the soldiers on deck stood irresolute, thinking the "boat's company were coming on board by Carver's invitation," and so permitted them to draw alongside. Whereupon Ludwell's men clambered in through the gun-room ports and rushed up on deck brandishing swords and pistols. One of them presented a pistol to Bland's breast, shouting: "You are my prisoner." At the same time Captain Larimore and his crew, seizing handspikes and other weapons, joined in the attack. The soldiers, taken completely by surprise, one of their commanders absent and the other captured, tamely laid down their arms.

In the meanwhile Carver, in the sloop, hearing the shouts and the clash of arms, tried to veer away from the ship and make his escape. But there was little wind, and before he could get well under way, Larimore trained his guns on him and threatened to sink him. So he and his men were captured. When Carver realized how he had been duped, "he stormed, tore his hair off and cursed, and exclaimed at the cowardice of Bland that had betrayed and lost all their designs."

The capture of Bland and Carver's fleet changed the whole situation. The Eastern Shore was no longer merely a place of refuge for the governor where he might hope temporarily to escape Bacon's conquering band, but a base of operations against all Virginia from the Potomac to the James. If Bacon concentrated his men in Gloucester, Berkeley might strike at Elizabeth City a few miles away across the York, but fifty or sixty miles away by land. If Bacon led his men around to Elizabeth City, he could strike at Gloucester, or perhaps Middlesex or Northumberland. Moreover, there was no hope that the patriots could regain their control of the water, for Berkeley's fleet grew larger with each incoming merchant ship from England. Bacon might continue to win temporary successes, he might repel every invasion from Northampton, but the stupidity of Bland and Carver in permitting Berkeley to trick and surprise them, had made ultimate success almost hopeless.

At "Arlington" there was exultation and renewed hope. Amid the toasts to Ludwell and Captain Larimore and cheers for the governor, plans were laid for an expedition up the James for the capture of Jamestown. To prepare the ground two men were sent over to York to arouse the people, undermine resistance and perhaps induce some to join the governor's forces. Berkeley had promised, they said, that all recruits should be rewarded from the estates of the "rebels," freed of all taxes for twenty-one years and paid at the rate of twelve pence a day, while those under indenture to any of Bacon's followers were to have their freedom. But this seems to have had little effect other than to throw the bewildered people into a panic. The planters hesitated to take up arms against the man who was defending them against both the Indians and the oppressions of the government, while they knew that Bacon might emerge at any moment from the forest to take quick revenge upon those who aligned themselves against him. On the other hand, they dreaded the savage cruelty of old Berkeley, who might confiscate their property or even lead them to the gallows. No wonder they looked upon themselves "as a people utterly undone," some wishing for Bacon's presence "as their only rock of safety," others fearing he would enmesh them in new and more treacherous quicksands.

But while the people of the mainland hesitated, preparations on the Eastern Shore were pushed vigorously for the expedition up the James. Ludwell sailed over to the mouth of York River and captured four sloops needed for transporting troops, and would have taken a small ship had she not been hauled up where he could not "come at her." Captain Gardiner sailed up in the *Adam and Eve* to place the ship and her crew at the governor's service.

So with the men raised in Accomac and Northampton, the refugees from the Western Shore and their servants, the crews of the merchantmen and Bland and Carver's men who had chosen service under the governor in preference to the gallows, some six or seven hundred men were got together, ready to embark. But it was a heterogeneous group, undisciplined, poorly armed, many of the men at heart with Bacon not the governor, others merely hoping for plunder. Berkeley was to find to his dismay that they were not to be relied upon when brought face to face with Bacon's veterans. But they made a martial appearance as they took their places in the sloops or rowed out to clamber aboard the larger vessels. So anchors were lifted, sails hoisted and the fleet, consisting of the *Rebecca*, the *Adam and Eve,* three smaller ships and sixteen sloops, moved across the bay, past Old Point Comfort and entered James River.

At the first sight of this formidable flotilla, horsemen galloped off to Jamestown, their hoofs "outstripping the canvas wings," to report the news to Colonel Thomas Hansford, the youthful commander of Bacon's forces in the capital. Now followed earnest consultations with Lawrence and Drummond. There were several hundred soldiers at Jamestown, but the fort had been stripped of cannon to arm the *Rebecca,* and it was doubtful whether the town could be defended against an attack by water. If the governor should land a force to cut off retreat past the Sandy Bay, while the ships opened upon the village itself, they might all be trapped and forced to surrender.

In the midst of this indecision the fleet hove in sight and anchored, while a boat came ashore with a promise of pardon for all save Lawrence and Drummond, if they would lay down their arms and make their submission.

Some were inclined to accept, for with Bacon far away their case seemed hopeless; others were skeptical of the governor's promise, "fearing to meet with some afterclaps of revenge." At last, unable to agree and almost defenseless, as night fell over the little capital they began a hurried flight, each man shifting for himself. Lawrence mounted his horse and rode off without pausing to gather up his valuables, even leaving "a fair cupboard of plate," glad to escape with his life.

The next morning at noon, the seventh of September 1676, the ships moved up to the town and Berkeley stepped ashore. There, in the presence of his followers, he fell on his knees to give thanks to God for the repossession of his capital. For one whose injustice, oppressions and blunders had driven the people into insurrection, and in whose heart there was a burning hatred for his opponents and an almost insane desire for revenge, this act would seem almost sacrilegious. But with Berkeley obedience to God and to the King were one and the same. The men who had resisted the authority of the King's representative, had done so not only at the risk of their necks but of their souls. In fighting them, hunting them down and punishing them he was not only serving the Throne but doing God's service. So we must think of him, not as a hypocrite but as a fanatical royalist.

Bacon emerged from the Dragon Swamp an ill man. His was not the constitution to withstand the hardships of fatiguing marches through woods and swamps, of frequent wettings from heavy rains, of hunger and improper food, of responsibilities and cares that might have broken the spirit of one less courageous and determined. One wonders whether he ever awoke in those nights in the Virginia forests to think of the security and comforts of Friston Hall, or of the little cottage in the Curles of the James where his wife prayed for his safe return. Perhaps he realized even then that death had laid its hand upon him and that for him there could be no more return to Suffolk or perhaps even to Henrico. It is the more remarkable, then, that he should have received the news of the capture of his little fleet, the loss of Jamestown and the dispersal of his forces there with such calmness and determination. He had with him but one hundred and thirty-six tired and half-starved men, while the governor's force, so he was informed, amounted to one thousand. It seemed hopeless to resist further.

Yet when he called his faithful veterans around him to tell them what had happened, they "cried out they would stand by their general to the last," and asked only that he lead them on against the enemy. Bacon was deeply moved.

"Gentlemen and fellow soldiers," he said, "how am I transported with gladness to find you thus unanimous, bold and daring, brave and gallant! You have the victory before you fight, the conquest before the battle! I know you can and dare fight, while they will lie in their place of refuge and dare not so much as appear in the field before you. Your hardiness will invite all the country along as we march to come in and second you.

"The Indians we bear along with us shall be as so many motives to cause relief from every hand to be brought to you. The infamous actions of our enemies cannot but so reflect upon their spirits, as they will have no courage left to fight you. I know you have the prayers and well-wishes of all the people in Virginia, while the others are loaded with their curses."

So the heroic little band set their faces toward Jamestown. As they trudged along over the roads of New Kent, past rail fences, "old fields," woods and plantations and through creeks, swamps and rivers, the people flocked out to greet them, shouting their praises, bringing them "fruits and victuals," praying for "their happiness" and denouncing the governor. Every now and then some sturdy planter, with his fusil or his pistol, perhaps on horseback, would approach Bacon and ask to be enrolled in his force. Even the women called out to him as he rode past that if he had need of them they too would enlist to fight beside their husbands. Everywhere the people were overjoyed at the sight of the sullen Indian captives whom he led along "as a show of triumph," which they accepted as an indication that he had effectually put an end to the raids on the plantations. The little army pitched camp in New Kent for a day or two in order to gather further recruits, while messengers were sent off to Henrico to arouse the people of the upper James.

Then, with his ranks swelled to three hundred men, Bacon moved swiftly down the left bank of the Chickahominy River into James City County and pitched camp at Green Spring "old fields" within a few miles of Jamestown. When word came to him that the governor's army was "well armed and resolute," he merely smiled, remarking, "I shall see that, for I am now going to try them." When another messenger reported that the governor had sent out a party of sixty horsemen to observe his movements, he remarked that they would be afraid to venture close enough to get any real information.

Despite this confidence, Bacon thought it wise to draw up his men and deliver another of those brief speeches which seem to have had always so profound an influence in arousing their enthusiasm and their love. "If ever you have fought well and bravely, you must do so now," he said. "They are fresh and unwearied, they have the advantage of position, they have a fortified town into which to retreat. But I speak not to discourage you, but to let you know what the advantages are which we shall wrest from them. They call us rebels and traitors, but we will see whether their courage is as great as their pretended loyalty. Come on, my hearts of gold, he who dies in the field of battle dies in the bed of honor."

And now as always, the sound of their young leader's voice inspired the little band with fresh determination and courage. As we look back through the mists of two and a half centuries and read between the lines of cold official documents, or the bitterly hostile letters of enemies, or the confessions of intimidated friends standing in the shadow of the gallows, Bacon emerges as a leader comparable even to George Washington or Robert E. Lee in his power to win and hold the love and confidence of his men.

As evening fell Bacon put his little army in motion, his vanguard some distance ahead of the main body, and headed for Jamestown driving before him a body of Berkeley's horse. Arriving at Colonel Francis Moryson's plantation, known formerly as Paspahegh Old Fields, opposite Sandy Bay, he rode out in front of his men within a short distance of the palisade across the isthmus where he discharged his carbine at the enemy and ordered his trumpeter to sound a defiant blast. Then he dismounted to look over the ground and make his preparations.

The sight which greeted him would have discouraged one less determined and resourceful. The only approach to the peninsula was well fortified, protected by three heavy guns no doubt taken from the ships, and guarded by a force far greater than his own. In the river was the fleet ready at a moment's notice to move up opposite the isthmus to open upon him should he attempt an assault. To the north the town was not only protected by the Back Creek, but by a series of marshes on both banks. There was no hope of reducing the place by starvation, as the ships and sloops gave ready access to Surry and Isle of Wight and kept open the line of communications with the Eastern Shore.

Yet Bacon began immediate preparations to reduce the place. Selecting a spot about three or four hundred feet from the palisades, he set his men to work making entrenchments. Although they had marched many miles that day, he kept them at work all night under the light of the moon, cutting down trees, clearing away bushes and throwing up earth. With the break of dawn Berkeley's watchers saw a little makeshift fortress before them, formidable only because of the desperate determination of the men who crouched within. As an evidence of their contempt for the enemy six of Bacon's men leapt over the parapet, rushed up to the palisade, fired upon the enemy and returned unharmed to their trenches.

Bacon and his men had imagined that Berkeley, with his overwhelming numbers, would at once sally out to storm their fort in the hope of routing them before the arrival of reinforcements. But Berkeley hesitated. He had every reason to distrust the loyalty of many of his men, he knew that Bacon's followers were desperate, he realized that the recent victory over the Indians made his young rival more than ever the idol of the people. So he gave orders that not a shot should be fired—with the hope, apparently, that Bacon would send in a message asking for reconciliation.

But Bacon did not trust the governor, remembering that Captain Carver, by listening to his fair promises, had merely put a noose around his own neck. When it was whispered through the camp that Berkeley might be willing to offer liberal terms of surrender, Bacon argued earnestly against it. "There is no trust to be reposed in our enemies, for they have shown themselves as treacherous as they are cowardly. And as for their reluctance to shedding blood, no longer ago than last week they fired against our men in an attempt to rob the stores provided for our supply in the Indian campaign."

When the governor realized that Bacon was resolved to fight, he made preparations to batter down his defenses before making a sally. The ships were brought as close in to the shore as possible where they opened with all their guns, while from the palisades came volley after volley from the fusils and carbines of the infantry. But Bacon's men, firing deliberately from behind their barrier of "trees, bush and earth," resolutely held their ground. In fact, they actually strengthened their position in the very heat of the engagement, for Bacon ordered each man to bind up a bundle of wood, and holding it against his breast as a shield from the enemy's fire, leap upon the parapet and place it on the earthwork.

In the meanwhile one of the sloops sailed bravely up into the comparatively shallow water close to Bacon's fort, where its crew opened fire, not only with shot but with "abundance of vaunting and railing expressions." When the patriots discovered that the commander was a certain Thomas Chamberlaine, a drunken, quarrelsome planter known personally to many of them, they began to jeer and ridicule him, and opened on him so deadly a fire that he was compelled to abandon the sloop and row off in a small boat.

Though Bacon's men came through the bombardment in good shape and stood resolute to repel a sally, their leader realized that his position would continue precarious until he had greatly enlarged and strengthened his works and protected them with heavy guns. But this would require time, while at any moment he might see Berkeley's men emerging from behind their palisades and storming across the open ground. So he hit upon a novel expedient to hold them at bay until he could get additional axes and spades to strengthen his fort and drag three guns across country to mount on it. Within a radius of a few miles were the plantations of some of Berkeley's chief henchmen where they had left not only their property but their families. Deciding to take advantage of this situation, Bacon sent out several small parties, galloping across country to capture and bring into his camp Elizabeth Page, wife of Colonel John Page, Angelica Bray, wife of Colonel James Bray, Anna Ballard, wife of

TORCHBEARER OF THE REVOLUTION

Colonel Thomas Ballard, Frances Thorpe, wife of Colonel Otho Thorpe and even Elizabeth Bacon, wife of his cousin Nathaniel Bacon, senior.

The poor ladies were terrified as the soldiers came riding up and ordered them to make hasty preparations to accompany them back to camp. As Elizabeth Bacon left King's Creek for that ten-mile ride across the peninsula, she must have thought of the strange course of events during the past two years which had converted the polished young man who had just arrived as a stranger from England, into a popular hero, the leader of a people in arms against their governor. She must have wondered also, what Bacon wanted with her, and whether he intended to subject her to insults or to injuries.

She was not long in finding out. Bacon assured her and the others that no harm was intended to them, but that they would be used to prevent an attack while his men were at work on the fort. One of them, perhaps Elizabeth Bacon herself, was conducted to the isthmus and instructed to enter the town and inform Berkeley that the others would be placed upon the ramparts where they would be exposed to imminent peril should his men sally out or even fire from the palisades and ships. It was with the deepest concern that the husbands received this news, and rushed to the palisades to wave to their wives as they stood on the ramparts and shout encouragement. So while the "white aprons," as they came to be called in history, remained as reluctant protectors, Bacon's men set to work busily, enlarging and strengthening their fort. And at last, when the great guns came up and were put in place to command the approach, Bacon pronounced all in readiness and gave orders to remove the ladies to a place of safety.

PROLOGUE TO THE REVOLUTION

The incident of the "white aprons," so inconsistent with his usual moderation, humanity and fairness, has brought much criticism upon Bacon. It can be excused only by the fact that he was at the time an ill man, worn down by excessive hardships, exertions and anxieties, who considered that he was dealing with an enemy as treacherous as he was cruel. He knew that if his little half-finished fort and his handful of faithful followers should fail to withstand an assault from the town and he himself fall into Berkeley's hand, he would be led to the scaffold within a few hours. He believed himself, as undoubtedly he was, the champion of the people against misrule and oppression, and he was embittered that he should be forced into the position of a rebel for freeing the colony of the deadly Indian menace. In such a cause and with such provocation he argued that any method of warfare was legitimate.

So now Bacon and his men stood at their posts awaiting the expected assault. Nearby was a solitary chimney, possibly all that was left of the old glassworks built in the days of the London Company, which commanded a view of the palisades and the ground beyond. One of Bacon's men climbed to the top to observe the number of Berkeley's men and report their movements. It was on September 15 that at last the sentinel called out that preparations were under way for the sally, and Bacon accordingly ordered every man to his post.

Minute after minute passed as the little army stood expectant and grim but the enemy failed to appear, until at the end of an hour the sentinel called out that they seemed to be breaking ranks. Thereupon Bacon ordered his men to relax their vigil.

At this moment when many of the patriots had left their posts, probably to retire to the camp, the gates of the palisade swung open and Berkeley's troops swarmed through to the attack.

Forming on the open ground where the isthmus broadened into the mainland, with those who had been forced to fight against their will in the van, they rushed forward. They came on, horse and foot, with a narrow front, "pressing very close upon one another's shoulders." But Bacon opened upon them at comparatively close range with such effect that they immediately threw down their arms and fled back to the palisades. The loyal men in the main division would probably have stood their ground had they not been borne back by the mad rush of the vanguard. It would have been better for Berkeley had he sent out his tried veterans to make the first assault, trusting to the freed indentured workers and his Accomac companies to support them and complete the victory. On the other hand, it is doubtful whether he had enough trustworthy men to make a vanguard, for in the end there were "only some twenty gentlemen willing to stand by him."

Although Bacon found a few dead stretched out before his trenches the battle was not bloody, thanks to the heels of the so-called loyalists. It was nonetheless decisive, for it showed Berkeley's men to be so utterly untrustworthy that they could not be relied upon to defend Jamestown. In fact, had Bacon yielded to his soldiers' entreaties to be permitted to follow them into the town, he might not only have captured the place, but Sir William and all of his supporters as well. It served no purpose for the old governor to revile his officers "in some passionate terms" for their failure; he might have anticipated his defeat from the "crabbed faces of his men" when the order to attack was delivered. A wit was prompted to say that a colonel's commission could be bought for the dottle of a pipe.

PROLOGUE TO THE REVOLUTION

The day after the unsuccessful sally, Bacon began a bombardment with his great guns, the one firing on the ships in the river, the other on the palisade, in order to effect a breach preparatory to an assault. In the town all was confusion. Rather than evacuate Jamestown, Berkeley would have preferred death on the spot, but with the "importunate and resistless solicitations of all he was at last overpersuaded, nay hurried away against his will." The little group of trusty gentlemen did all in their power to stem the tide, but they too were powerless in the face of the panic-stricken troops. When the shades of night veiled the movements in town from Bacon's watchers, hasty preparations were made for embarkation. The great guns were spiked, stores of arms, ammunition, and household goods—silver, clothing, utensils—were moved to the landing and taken on board the ships, the soldiers and townspeople following and the little fleet, weighing anchor, slipped silently down stream.

There can be no better evidence of the unpopularity of Berkeley's cause than this base desertion of the capital. The place, surrounded as it was by water save for an isthmus thirty feet wide, protected by swamps, defended by heavily armed ships and a force far greater than Bacon's, was practically impregnable. Berkeley should have been able to hold it, if only with his handful of faithful gentlemen and the English sailors from the *Rebecca* and the *Adam and Eve*. But the vast majority of his men seem to have been at heart with Bacon and so proved a liability rather than an asset. The governor, by long years of oppression and injustice had so alienated the people who had once respected and even loved him, that in all Virginia not one man in a hundred would lift a hand to defend him save from compulsion and fear.

The next morning, it being September 19, just twelve days after the landing of Sir William, Bacon's men marched triumphantly into the town. A very different aspect it presented from that day three months before when many of the same men had followed their leader over the great road to the State House green. Then all was bustle and stir, with the Assembly in session, the taverns full and crowds following the troops to see the show. Now the village was silent, the people gone, the houses empty. A diligent search revealed only a few horses, a great many tanned hides, some Indian corn and two or three cellars of wine.

Having gained possession of Jamestown, Bacon was uncertain as to what he should do with it. Calling a conference of his advisers, possibly in the Council chamber of the State House, possibly in Lawrence's residence, he laid the military situation before them and asked their advice. That he was uneasy as to conditions in Lancaster, Northumberland and Westmoreland is shown by his letter, written two days before to Captain William Cookson and Captain Edward Skewon, two of his lieutenants, urging them to "encourage the soldiers in the upper parts and let them know what a pitiful enemy we have to deal with." So he was not surprised when the news reached him that his former supporter, Colonel Giles Brent, who had gone over to the governor's party, had raised a thousand men in the northern counties and was marching south to attack him.

The little group of determined men decided that Jamestown was untenable. Should Brent close in on them from the north, blocking escape past Sandy Beach, while Berkeley's fleet moved back up the river to bombard them with the great guns and cut off communications by water, they would be trapped. The governor would have to wait only a short while until their provisions gave out to force them to surrender at will. On the other hand, if they evacuated the place to go out against Brent, Berkeley would reoccupy it, fortify it more strongly than ever, and the fruits of their victory would be lost. Had their army been stronger they might have divided it, leaving one division to guard Jamestown and sending out the other against Brent. But it was imperative that Bacon keep together the force at his command, outnumbered as it was by both of the "loyal" armies.

With grave faces and sinking hearts the patriots decided to burn Jamestown.

As the only town in Virginia and the capital of the colony, it was dear to them all. Here was the State House, here the famous brick church, here some of them had their residences and had spent a large part of their lives. But they were determined that when Berkeley returned he should find only smouldering timbers and blackened brick walls. Bacon with his own hands set fire to the church, which might have been converted into a barracks by the enemy. Lawrence rushed across Back Street to burn his own residence while Drummond applied the torch to his. Nothing was spared. Fortunately, Drummond ran into the State House, and conveyed the colonial records to a place of safety or they would have been destroyed. It was a sight never before seen in Virginia, as the flames enveloped one quaint little house after another, and sent up sparks into the darkness of the night. If there were any in Bacon's band who had seen the great London fire of ten years before they must have smiled at the comparison, but for the others the sight was awe-inspiring. Twenty-five houses were destroyed, five of them owned by Berkeley himself, including the State House block, the village proper, and all the outlying residences.

TORCHBEARER OF THE REVOLUTION

It was a daring deed, the act of desperate men, this burning of Jamestown, the forerunner of similar great sacrifices in Virginia's later revolutions—the burning of Norfolk in 1776 by the patriots to prevent its occupation by the British, and the partial burning of Richmond in 1865 upon its evacuation by the Confederate army.

As for Governor Berkeley, he cursed the cowardice of his soldiers as he stood on the deck of his ship and saw in the sky and reflected in the water the glare of burning buildings. He was too stubborn to admit that it was his own mistakes, his avarice, his hatred of republican principles, his contempt for private rights, which had brought this humiliation upon him. To him it seemed the act of wicked and rebellious men, which could easily have been averted had his own soldiers done their duty. But since there was no longer any reason for lingering in the James River, he weighed anchor and slipped down stream, while on shore parties of Bacon's horse kept pace to watch his movements and prevent the sailors from landing to entrench themselves or to seek water and provisions. Turning into Hampton Roads the fleet rounded Point Comfort and headed across the bay to Northampton.

On September 20, Bacon's forces donned their helmets, shouldered their fusils, halberds and carbines, and turning their backs upon the blackened walls and gaunt chimneys of Jamestown, marched over to Green Spring. Here Bacon remained several days, making his headquarters in the governor's residence and feeding his army at the expense of his estate. Then he set his columns in motion across the peninsula to the neighborhood of the present Yorktown, and transported them over the York River to Tindal's Point, now Gloucester Point.

Hardly had he established himself at "Warner Hall," in Gloucester County, the residence of Berkeley's friend

PROLOGUE TO THE REVOLUTION

Colonel Augustine Warner, than a messenger came riding up posthaste with the information that Brent's army, numbering one thousand men, horse and foot, had reached Rappahannock County and was advancing rapidly upon him. It was a dangerous situation. Unless Bacon could defeat Brent, Berkeley would bring his ships into the York and the Rappahannock and block him up within the limits of Gloucester and Middlesex Counties.

He met the new peril with characteristic decision. Drawing up his men under their colors, he explained the situation and asked them if they were ready to go out against this new enemy. If he had any doubt of their loyalty and determination he was reassured by their shouts and acclamations. Unburdening themselves of all save the most necessary equipment, his veterans wheeled into line while the "drums thundered out the march."

This time Bacon advanced in easy stages, so that his men would be fresh when they came in contact with the enemy. But there was no battle. When Brent's men heard that the veterans of the Occaneechee and Pamunkey campaigns were approaching they refused to fight and, deserting their officers, returned to their homes. At heart many of them were in sympathy with Bacon, and saw no reason why they should risk their lives to reestablish the governor's power. Brent was dismayed at the desertion of his men, complaining that they had "forsaken the stoutest man and ruined the fairest estate in Virginia," now left to the "mercy of the Baconians."

But for the moment Bacon was more concerned with organizing Virginia, and in binding the people to his cause before the arrival of the redcoats, than in plundering Brent's estate. We suspect that it was Lawrence's subtle pen which drew up a new oath of fidelity which the people were asked to take, but there are several fiery passages in Bacon's true style. This paper recited that Berkeley had in a barbarous and abominable manner exposed the lives of the people and hindered their efforts to defend themselves against the Indians, that when Bacon's men went out to fight them, he raised troops to attack them in the rear. When the people defeated this bloody design he left the country and for the moment it was not known to what parts of the world he did repair. The oath continued:

We protest against him as a traitor and enemy of the public and we swear that we will oppose and prosecute him by every means in our power. Moreover, since he has plotted to ruin this poor colony by setting the heart of our sovereign against us by false information, has intercepted our messages, prevented our sending our agents to England in the people's behalf and requested his Majesty to send troops to subdue us, we swear that we will first treat with the commander of these forces and if he will not come to an understanding with us, we will fly together in our own defense as in a common calamity to stand and fall with General Bacon and his forces. We are resolved to fight the troops and if reduced to the last extremity, when we can no "longer defend ourselves, our lives and liberties," we will desert our homes and the colony rather than submit to such unheard of injustice.

It was late in September or early in October that the Gloucester trained bands assembled at the courthouse at Bacon's command. When they were drawn up to the number of six or seven hundred men Bacon addressed them at some length, urging them to take the new oath. But the Gloucestermen hesitated. They were thankful to Bacon for delivering them from the Indian peril, they had no love for the governor, but they dared not defy the King by opposing his soldiers in arms. Gloucester, situated as it was on deep water, would be almost defenseless against an army supported by a naval squadron. So a certain Mr. Cole stood forth as spokesman for the Gloucestermen, giving their objections to taking the oath and requesting that they be permitted to remain neutral.

It was a severe blow to Bacon, this clear evidence that he did not have the unanimous support of the people. They had been willing to have him go out against the savages at the risk of his life, to force through the Assembly a series of liberal laws for their benefit, but they refused to stand by him in the hour of his greatest peril. It must have been a deep humiliation to the Gloucestermen when the slender, dark-haired young man reproached them for this desertion. He said they were like the worst of sinners, who wish to be saved with the righteous and yet do nothing to obtain salvation. As he was turning away in disgust, one of his officers reminded him that he had spoken only to the horse and not the infantry. But Bacon, disappointed, apprehensive of the future, an ill man, replied testily that he had spoken to the men, not to the horses. When he learned that the Reverend James Wadding, of Petsworth parish, Gloucester, not only had refused to take the oath but had done his best to dissuade others from subscribing, he put him under arrest. "It is your place to preach in the church, not in the camp," he said. "In church you may say what you please, in camp you will say what I please, unless you can fight to better purpose than you can preach."

For the first time, Bacon now began to show a more "merciless severity and absolute authority," plundering the estates of some of his opponents, arresting others, trying them by court-martial and committing them to prison. James Wilkenson, a deserter, was condemned to death and executed. "This we look on to be more an act of his policy than cruelty," it was afterwards reported to the King, "to prevent and awe others from deserting him, we not observing him to have been bloodily inclined in the whole progress of the rebellion."

Among others who faced Bacon's court were the Reverend John Clough, minister of Jamestown, Captain Thomas Hawkins, junior, of Rappahannock and Major John West of New Kent. When a plea for mercy was made for these three men, Bacon expressed a willingness to exchange them for Carver, Bland and others held captive by Sir William. And though this was not done, none of the three was ever executed. Yet Bacon's greater severity had the effect of putting a temporary end to open opposition in Gloucester so that when he summoned the militia to a second meeting, they all subscribed to the oath and pledged themselves to oppose the British troops.

But Bacon knew the uses of moderation as well as of severity, for he wished the people to judge between the mildness of his own conduct and Berkeley's harshness. When his soldiers began to browbeat inoffensive planters and plunder their plantations, it could only alienate them from his cause and drive them into the enemy's camp. So he instituted a rigid discipline, calling his men strictly to account when reports came to him of plundering done without his orders. And instead of hanging every prominent enemy who fell into his hands he released some of them before trial and pardoned others who had been condemned. On the other hand, it was necessary to feed his army and food was to be had only from the neighboring plantations. The estates of Berkeley's supporters were the first to suffer and many were the complaints of cattle, sheep, hogs, Indian corn, wheat, blankets, clothing, etc. carried off by the "rebels."

PROLOGUE TO THE REVOLUTION

In order to lighten the tremendous burden of responsibility which rested upon his shoulders, Bacon now began to organize several committees to aid him in keeping order, carrying on civil affairs and waging the war. To one was intrusted the affairs on the south side of James River, with the special duty of inquiring into the plundering which was going on there. Another was to accompany the army in its expeditions, to have jurisdiction over seizures and call the men to account for "rudeness, disorder, spoil and waste." The third was to manage the Indian war.

It was also imperative that Bacon should turn his attention to the Eastern Shore. None better than he realized the tremendous advantage to Berkeley in having a base where he was safe from attack and from which he could attack at will. If Bacon divided his forces to garrison important posts along the banks of the rivers, Sir William might surprise them one after another and capture them all. If he concentrated his army in one place, the enemy might overrun whole counties before he could march around the heads of the rivers to oppose them. He must have rued the folly of Carver and Bland in permitting the governor to outwit them and secure possession of their little fleet, for with the *Rebecca* and a flotilla of sloops at his command he could easily have crossed the bay to come to grips with the same men who had fled before him at Jamestown.

It is stated by one chronicler that Bacon in October was planning to invade the Eastern Shore, but he leaves us in the dark as to how he expected to get there. To march through Maryland around the head of Chesapeake Bay and then down to Accomac and Northampton was out of the question. Nor could Bacon have contemplated building a fleet in which to transport his men, for this would have been a matter of many months, while the English warships were expected within a few weeks.

There is some evidence that he did send over a small party, probably under cover of night, to rally the people of the Eastern Shore to his standard, for Berkeley afterward reported that Captain George Farloe, "one of Cromwell's soldiers, very active in this rebellion," came with forty men "to surprise me at Accomac." But Farloe was captured perhaps by the armed ships before he got across the bay, and like so many of Bacon's lieutenants ended his days on the scaffold.

Bacon's real offensive against Berkeley's place of refuge was the drawing up of an appeal to the people of the Eastern Shore, by which he hoped to turn them against the governor and perhaps even to put him under restraint. But this paper was ill suited to its purpose. It should have been mild and persuasive in tone, praising the people of Accomac and Northampton for their reluctance to fight under Berkeley, dwelling upon his many oppressions and promising to assist them in throwing off his yoke. Instead, it took a tone of censure and of threat. It was base and sordid, Bacon told them, to invade the mainland and "be the first beginners of bloodshed . . . for hopes of plunder." But though their consciences no doubt pricked them, he could excuse them as the dupes of the governor, whose passion and folly had involved the colony in such a "labyrinth of ruin."

If fifteen days after the arrival of this paper he added, you send some of your discreet persons to make us satisfaction for your piracies and deliver up the ringleader to be sent to England for trial and immediately return those of our party whom you hold prisoners, then we will treat with you as brothers and friends. Otherwise can you blame us if we prosecute you with all extremity of war?

PROLOGUE TO THE REVOLUTION

Apparently this manifesto had no effect. If it ever reached the Eastern Shore it was no doubt confiscated by the governor's followers and so remained unknown to the mass of the people. But even though rumors of its contents might have been whispered among the troops or spread from plantation to plantation, it could not alter the fact that Bacon in Gloucester might just as well have been in Africa so far as carrying out the threats was concerned, whereas the English warships were probably already on their way to lend irresistible force to the governor.

Possibly Bacon hoped to break Berkeley's hold on the Eastern Shore through the spread of his movement into Maryland. In his conversation with John Goode he showed that he was acquainted with the deep dissatisfaction of the people north of the Potomac, even going so far as to say they hoped ultimately for independence. To what extent Bacon was in communication with the malcontents in Maryland and North Carolina we do not know, but it was undoubtedly by emulation of his movement, if not actually at his instigation, that the people of Calvert County rose in arms in September 1676.

Driven to desperation by poverty resulting from the Navigation Acts and angered by the oppressions of the proprietary government, William Davis, John Pate, William Gent and Giles Hasleham drew up a paper protesting against the encroachments upon "the liberties of the freemen of Maryland." In answer to their summons sixty men assembled in arms on the banks of the Patuxent to extort from the governor and Council "certain immunities and freedoms." When the governor commanded them to lay down their arms they defied him, and "marched away with drums beating and colors flying."

But the movement in Maryland lacked coordination and leadership. Had Davis and Pate acted in conjunction with Josias Fendall and John Code, whom Lord Baltimore termed "two rank Baconists," they might have gained the mastery of the colony. Then it might have been possible to ferry over from Calvert County to the Eastern Shore a force of cavalry strong enough to descend on Accomac and Northampton and force Berkeley to seek refuge on board his fleet. But Fendall and Code hesitated, Baltimore's forces under Thomas Notley dispersed the insurgents, Davis and Pate were captured and hanged, and the opportunity was lost for Bacon.

Upon North Carolina Bacon reposed his hopes even more than upon Maryland, declaring that the people there "were resolved to own their governor no further" and nominating "Carolina" as his watchword. Unfortunately for him, the actual uprising on Albemarle Sound did not occur until October 1677, nearly a year after his death and eight or nine months after the suppression of his followers. But the close relationship of the two movements is obvious. The Carolinians, like the Virginians, were impoverished by the restraint on their trade, like the Virginians they were denied a free election of their representatives in Assembly, their leaders, like Bacon, were accused of "laboring industriously to be popular" and of poisoning the colony with complaints against the provincial government.

Had Bacon lived to take advantage of the discontent in Maryland and Carolina by uniting those colonies with Virginia under his authority, he might have caused England serious trouble. With the entire Chesapeake Bay region behind him he could have put two thousand well-equipped cavalrymen in the field to cope with the forces coming over from England. He might have made it difficult for the redcoats to effect a landing or to provision the ships, he might have cut off small parties or garrisons and have delayed indefinitely the subjugation of the region.

But this was not to be. While the effects of exposure and overexertion were beginning to tell on his constitution and lower his vitality, he made his last strategic move in the game of war with the governor by concentrating most of his troops at the plantation of Major Thomas Pate on Portopotank Creek, in Gloucester, a few miles east of West Point. Here he was in position to defend not only the region between the York and the Rappahannock but the peninsula and even the Northern Neck. Possibly he planned to keep his main force at this point in anticipation of an invasion from the Eastern Shore, while bodies of cavalry patrolled the Northern Neck, the south side of James River and perhaps the lower peninsula. But we can only conjecture as to his plans, for while he was at Pate's house his illness became so serious that he was compelled to take to his bed.

We do not know who was the physician who attended Bacon in his last illness. It is to be hoped that his wife was at his bedside to add her loving care to the ministrations of Drummond and Lawrence and his other devoted followers. Bacon was not a deeply religious man, but now, with the hand of death upon him, he summoned Mr. Wadding, possibly from the prison in which he had placed him, to prepare his mind for death. As he became weaker and his fever rose, his mind dwelt upon the perils of the people for whom he had made such great sacrifices and upon the hopelessness of his own situation. Now and then he would arouse himself to inquire whether the guard around the house was strong, or whether the English frigates had arrived. He died October 26, 1676.

Certain historians have attached some mystery to Bacon's death, one actually going so far as to suggest that

Berkeley had him poisoned. But the various accounts leave no doubt that he was a victim of dysentery, brought on by excessive fatigue, exposure to the weather in the Dragon Swamp and the trenches before Jamestown and by improper diet. His enemies made much of the fact that during his illness he was infected with lice, so that his shirts had be be burned "as often as he shifted himself," and it is to this, undoubtedly, that an act of Assembly referred when it spoke of his death as being "infamous." But there is no reason to believe that the lice, a natural accompaniment of his marches in the forests, actually contributed to his death. It is obvious that this young Englishman of slender frame, accustomed to the life of an English manor and not yet acclimated to Virginia, was not strong enough to endure hardships which might have undermined the strongest constitution—forced marches, hunger, sleep in the open under the forest trees, exposure to heavy rains, violent disputes, weighty responsibilities, apprehensions for himself, his family and the people who had reposed their trust in him. Bacon is as truly a martyr to American freedom as Nathan Hale or Hugh Mercer.

The announcement that their leader was dead fell upon the patriot camp like a pronouncement of doom. What hope was left now that their hero was gone? Who could lead them against the Indians, who defend their liberties, who save them from the revenge of the infuriated governor, who rescue the colony from chaos? The disposal of the body is shrouded in mystery. It was whispered through Virginia in after months that Lawrence in the dead of night had removed the remains of his friend to some hidden spot for burial, so that Berkeley, when he disinterred the casket used at the funeral found it empty save for stones. In this way was he cheated of the satisfaction of exposing the body on the gibbet.

In the official papers of the colony Bacon is never mentioned after his death save in terms of opprobrium as traitor, rebel, impostor, seducer of the people. He was linked to Oliver Cromwell as the enemy of the country and King. But in many a humble home his name was revered as long as any remained who remembered him or had served under him. To the men who followed him into the wilderness, or fought beside him in the trenches at Sandy Beach, or saw him beard the old governor on the green before the State House he was always the hero, the martyr. His praises were even sung in verse, much of it crude no doubt, but all having the merit of deep sincerity. The one short poem which has come down to us, entitled "Bacon's Epitaph, made by his Man," is perhaps the finest bit of verse which we have from the entire colonial period.

>   Death why so cruel! What, no other way
> To manifest thy spleene, but thus to slay
> Our hopes of safety, liberty, our all
> Which, through thy tyranny, with him must fall
> To its late chaos? Had thy rigid force
> Been dealt by retail, and not thus in gross
> Grief had been silent: Now we must complain
> Since thou, in him, hast more than thousand slain
> Whose lives and safeties did so much depend
> On him their life, with him their lives must end.
>   If't be a sin to think Death brib'd can be
> We must be guilty: say 'twas bribery
> Guided the fatal shaft. Virginia's foes,
> To whom for secret crimes just vengeance owes
> Deserved plagues, dreading their just desert
> Corrupted Death by Paracelsian art
> Him to destroy; whose well tried courage such,
> Their heartless hearts, nor arms, nor strength could touch.

TORCHBEARER OF THE REVOLUTION

   Who now must heal those wounds, or stop that blood
The Heathen made, and drew into a flood?
Who is't must plead our cause? nor trump nor Drum
Nor deputations, these alas are dumb
And cannot speak. Our arms (though ne'er so strong)
Will want the aid of his commanding tongue,
Which conquered more than Caesar: He overthrew
Only the outward frame; this could subdue
The rugged works of nature. Souls replete
With dull chilled cold, he'd animate with heat
Drawn forth of reason's Lymbick. In a word
Mars and Minerva both in him concurred
For arts, for arms, whose sword and pen alike,
As Cato's did, may admiration strike
In to his foes; while they confess withall
It was their guilt stil'd him a criminal.
Only this difference doth from truth proceed:
They in the guilt, he in the name must bleed,
While none shall dare his obsequies to sing
In deserv'd measures, until time shall bring
Truth crown'd with freedom, and from danger free,
To sound his praises to posterity.

CHAPTER VI
LIBERTY DEFERRED

"WITH HIM THEIR LIVES MUST END"

Liberty Deferred

THE VIRGINIA POET SPOKE TRULY WHEN HE SAID THAT Bacon's army "though ne'er so strong will want the aid of his commanding tongue." There was no one to take his place. The troops might find in their ranks someone whose experience on the battlefields of Europe fitted him to take control of military affairs, but it would be too much to expect him to have also the qualities necessary for reorganizing the government, keeping open the courts and maintaining order. Was there a man in all Virginia who, like Bacon, had turned his back on the highest honors and the greatest opportunities for personal aggrandizement that he might champion the people's cause? Could another take his place in their affections, or keep them united and steadfast in the struggle for liberty, or strike such swift and telling blows, or so quickly bring order out of chaos? Either Lawrence or Drummond might have been a wise choice had they not been ignorant of military affairs, or Thomas Hansford, had he had more experience in important civil offices.

It is not true, as many historians have stated, that the whole movement collapsed as soon as fate removed Bacon from the scene, for the marches, battles and raids continued for several months, and it was only in January that Berkeley regained his authority over the Virginia mainland. Yet without Bacon's hand this early ship of American liberty drifted aimlessly until finally it went upon the rocks. The patriots became divided "into several parties and opinions," their leaders could not prevent the troops from pillaging, the civil government to all intents was nonexistent, there was a lack of cohesion and unity in the military plans. The people were as bitterly angry as ever with Berkeley, they were as ready to defend their rights, but they were helpless without a real leader and in the end were forced to bend their necks to the yoke.

But for the present there was no thought of submission. Joseph Ingram was chosen to lead the army, and as he stood before the troops hat in hand while a herald read his commission, the men bravely cheered him, shouting: "God save our new general!" We know little of Ingram save that, like Bacon, he was a recent arrival in the country, that he claimed the title of esquire and that he married a rich Virginia widow. He is ridiculed by one of the Virginia chroniclers as an ape trying to take the lion's place, a "milksop" who could dance well upon a rope, but one suspects that this harsh judgment was not entirely deserved. Ingram, though obviously not of the caliber of Bacon, showed a promptness of decision, a courage and a knowledge of military affairs which made him more than a match for Berkeley's commanders.

Bacon, with the instinct of the true strategist, had already selected West Point, where the Pamunkey and the Mattapony unite to form the York, as his headquarters and his main point of concentration, and Ingram now proceeded to put this plan into operation. Here he was within a day's march of the Rappahannock on the north, of the James on the south, of York County on one side of the York River, of Gloucester on the other and of the frontier. Had he supplemented this step with the creation of a flying body of cavalry, ready at a moment's notice to descend upon any party of invaders from the

LIBERTY DEFERRED

Eastern Shore, he might have held the governor at bay until the arrival of the English fleet. It would have been easy for his watchers, the moment they saw the white sails of Sir William's ships heading for the mouth of the York or the James, to send up smoke signals, and a few minutes later Ingram's horse would have gone thundering across country to prevent a landing.

On the other hand, the policy of scattering small groups over the country was an open invitation to Berkeley to overpower them singly. Ingram posted about a hundred men at Green Spring under Captain Drew to guard the north bank of James River and maintain themselves at the expense of the governor's cattle and corn. He attached such importance to this post that he brought here three great guns, fortified all approaches, and gave orders that it should be defended to the end. On the south side of James River the patriots made their headquarters at the residence of Major Arthur Allen, a quaint two-story brick house, with Flemish gable ends and high Tudor chimney stacks, still standing amid the fields and woods of Surry as a lonely reminder of the struggles and suffering of the men who fought for the cause of American liberty more than two and a half centuries ago. Here Major William Rookings stood guard with a "considerable number" of resolute men.

On the York, Major Thomas Whaley, described as "a stout ignorant fellow," was in command of about forty men, most of them pressed into service, at the residence of the elder Nathaniel Bacon, on King's Creek. Lower down the river, in the house formerly occupied by Colonel George Reade on the site of Yorktown, was stationed Captain Thomas Hansford, one of the bravest of Bacon's followers, a true patriot and a man of high and noble spirit. Another group took possession of Mr.

185

William Howard's house in Gloucester, another fortified itself in the residence of Colonel John Washington, in Westmoreland County, and still others in various isolated posts.

This policy was probably forced on Ingram, partly by the demand of all sections for protection, partly by the difficulty of supplying by land transit a large force concentrated in one place. At this time bulky commodities were conveyed from one part of the colony to another almost entirely in sloops or other small vessels, for the whole tidewater region was intersected by innumerable rivers and creeks. The roads, which ran usually on the ridges between the rivers so as to avoid the necessity of crossing small streams, were merely enlarged Indian trails, narrow, poorly graded and quite unfit for heavy traffic. Consequently, although almost every planter had his boat, very few indeed had wagons. Even Braddock, eighty years later could not find in Virginia enough large wagons for his expedition against Fort Duquesne, so it is not surprising that for Bacon's men the problem of transportation became almost hopeless the moment Berkeley secured control of the water. Ingram might have driven cattle and sheep to West Point in sufficient numbers to sustain his army, but it would have been difficult to supply wheat, corn, fruit or vegetables. On the other hand, in scattered garrisons the troops could and did help themselves from the estates of the governor's friends, using up their wheat and corn and slaughtering their livestock. Before the uprising had collapsed they had stripped Sir William himself, Colonel Bacon, Arthur Allen, Otho Thorpe, Colonel John West, Colonel Augustine Warner, Colonel Daniel Parke and many others.

But whatever the motives for dividing the army into isolated garrisons, events immediately showed how fatal a policy it was. It was probably early in November that a strong force under Major Robert Beverley clambered aboard a little fleet of transports and, hoisting sail, headed across the bay for the mouth of the York River. It must have been night when they moved in past what is now Light Point, for no one gave the alarm to the garrisons higher up stream. So, when they landed at the site of Yorktown to swoop down upon the Reade house, the patriots were taken by surprise and put to rout. Hansford was captured, hustled down to the boats and taken over to the Eastern Shore to await his trial for treason. Greatly encouraged by this success, Beverley came back into York River a few days later to duplicate his performance. This time he captured Major Edmund Cheeseman, together with Captain Thomas Wilford, "a little man but no coward," who had served Bacon as interpreter in the Indian war.

Having now in his clutches six of the leaders in the uprising, and encouraged by Bacon's death and the obvious incapacity of his successor, Berkeley began a series of trials and executions unparalleled in all American history for brutality and vindictiveness. The hanging of witches in New England was the result of religious fervor mingled with superstitious fear; Berkeley's hangings can be explained only as the revenge of a merciless old man. The plea that he was performing what he believed to be his duty to the King is untenable in view of the fact that he actually defied the King himself when Charles ordered him to issue a proclamation pardoning all save Bacon. Some writers have idealized Berkeley as the "Cavalier" governor; but he should go down in history as Berkeley the Executioner.

The first native-born Virginian to die upon the scaffold was Thomas Hansford. As he stood before the governor and a few of his followers who constituted what Berkeley called a Council of War, and listened to their verdict of guilty and the sentence of death upon the gallows, he neither flinched nor asked for mercy. Yet he did plead passionately that he might be shot like a soldier and not hanged like a dog. But you are not condemned for being a soldier, Sir William replied, but as a rebel taken in arms against the King, so that you must suffer the death the law prescribes for rebellion. So this martyr to the cause of American freedom prepared himself to die by professing repentance for all his sins "excepting rebellion which he would not acknowledge." And as he stood on the scaffold before the people of the Eastern Shore who had gathered around to witness the gruesome spectacle, he made a brief address declaring that he had taken up arms only for the defense of Virginia against the Indians and that he died a loyal subject and a lover of his country.

Major Cheeseman died in prison before his trial, but not before he had felt the malice and cruelty of the governor in a way calculated to inflict the deepest wound. When he was brought a prisoner to the Eastern Shore, Berkeley demanded sternly why he had taken up arms against the King. Before he could reply his wife rushed in and falling on her knees, pleaded that since it was at her instigation he had joined Bacon, she might be hanged and he pardoned. It was not to be expected that Berkeley would grant this request of a woman distracted with grief and apprehension, but it was certainly not consistent with the "Cavalier" spirit to scorn her with the worst of insults.

To Captain Wilford fate was less kind and this man, the second son of a knight who had lost life and estate in fighting for Charles I, was sent to the scaffold by the man who acted in the name of Charles II.

LIBERTY DEFERRED

When George Farloe came before the court-martial he pleaded that he had joined Bacon only when he gave him a commission signed by the governor himself. He had acted also in obedience to the General Assembly and if he had not obeyed Bacon he could have been tried and hanged. But the court pointed out that his commission was for service against the Indians only. Search your commission, they said, to see whether it gave you permission to take up arms against the governor's authority and person. Farloe rejoined that Bacon was authorized in his commission to see that the King's peace was kept. Do you then think, the court asked sarcastically, that the way to keep the King's peace was to resist the King's governor and levy war on him? Be silent, while sentence is pronounced on you.

Farloe's death excited great regret, for he was known as a man of peaceful disposition, a good scholar and much beloved. The hanging of John Johnson, described by Berkeley as "a stirrer up of the people but no fighter," completed the executions on the Eastern Shore.

Elated with his successes, Berkeley now planned an invasion of Gloucester County, hoping that the people would rise in arms to support him. He had word that the plundering by Ingram's men and the apprehension of an invasion by the English troops were rapidly turning sentiment in his favor. Embarking a force of one hundred and fifty men on four ships and two or three sloops, he set sail for the York River. Arriving there, he dispatched Beverley on another of his sudden raids, this time against the house of William Howard, garrisoned by a small party under a certain John Harris. Beverley surrounded the house in the early hours of the morning, and finding the defenders asleep, captured them all. Not content with hastening his prisoners away to the boats, he raided

Howard's plantation and store to help provision the fleet and reward his men.

In the meanwhile Major Lawrence Smith and a minister, no doubt the Reverend James Wadding, raised the governor's standard at the very house where Bacon had died and summoned all loyal subjects to assemble there. The Gloucester men had no more desire to fight for Sir William now than on former occasions, but they feared that to ignore this call might subject them to the charge of rebellion and bring disaster to themselves and their county when the redcoats arrived. So Smith found himself in command of a force which had their resolution been equal to their numbers could have "beaten all the rebels in the country only with their axes and hoes." At the same time the militia of Middlesex, across the Piankitank directly north of Gloucester, were likewise summoned to the colors although they too had no heart in fighting for the governor. For the moment, however, it seemed that Ingram would be overwhelmed.

But the patriots were as resolute as ever, were as determined not to yield to the governor, not to permit him to restore the old oppressive régime. So they struck with all the vigor and determination of the days when Bacon led them to one victory after another. Sir William's halfhearted recruits fled at their approach and when Ingram sent Gregory Wakelett, his second in command, out from West Point with a body of horse to regain Middlesex, he found that the enemy had vanished.

Major Smith's forces for the moment presented a more resolute front, for they stood their ground as Ingram approached with Bacon's veterans and for a few minutes it seemed that a decisive battle was imminent. At this moment a certain Major Bristow, stepping out of the ranks of the loyal army, offered to "try the equity and justness" of the governor's cause in a single combat with any champion in Ingram's force. Thereupon Ingram himself, swearing he would be the man, advanced on foot with sword and pistol. But his men, who had so recently lost one leader and had no wish to risk another in a foolish duel, caught him by the arm and brought him back.

As for Smith's recruits, they were far from having the belligerent spirit of their champion and asked nothing better than an opportunity to avoid a conflict with the resolute men who now faced them. Despite the desperate efforts of their leaders they opened negotiations with Ingram and agreed to lay down their arms on condition that they be permitted to return to their homes. No less than six hundred men thus tamely surrendered. Major Smith and some of his officers made good their escape, but many others fell into Ingram's hands and were taken to West Point in triumph.

These reverses for the governor were followed by another equally disappointing. The sudden raids upon the isolated posts of the insurgents had hitherto been so successful that it was now decided to surprise the garrison at Colonel Bacon's house on King's Creek. Selecting the usual early hour, Captain Hubert Farrill landed with one hundred and twenty men, and tried to steal up on the residence in the dark. With him was Colonel Bacon himself to point out the various approaches and the best means of attack. It was planned to drive in the sentries and before the garrison could seize their arms to "enter pell mell with them into the house." But at the first sound of firing the defenders rushed to arms and opened so deadly a fire that they forced Farrill's men to seek shelter behind the outbuildings. Later, when the garrison sallied out, the attackers lost their courage and fled back to their boats, leaving behind their leader, who was found dead, his commission "dropping-wet with blood in his pocket."

Despite the complete failure of Berkeley's York River campaign, it became obvious that the patriot cause was on the wane. Had there been a real government with the authority to levy taxes with which to pay the officers and men and purchase supplies, Ingram could easily have held his own. But he had no other way of feeding his troops than by confiscating the property of nearby planters, in some cases friends as well as foes. At the same time the difficulty of communication led to the disintegration of the forces, since garrisons on the lower James or the upper Potomac were so cut off from Ingram that they were forced to act independently. So, with the heroic young leader around whom the movement had centered removed by death, with the country fast falling into chaos, with neighbors pillaging each other, with the approach of cold weather increasing the sufferings of the people, with the English troops expected daily, the hopes of the men who had rushed to arms to defend their lives and their liberties sank to the lowest ebb. There were many who would rather have died than bend the neck, but the mass of the people were ready to lay down their arms and sullenly, bitterly submit once more to the will of the tyrannical old governor.

They were all the more discouraged when they found that the weapon of economic pressure was to be applied against them. The watchers at Old Point had seen one sail after another appear over the water, as the merchant vessels from England came in with sorely needed supplies of manufactured goods. If they could induce the masters to land their boxes of clothing, farm implements, medicines, arms, household utensils, etc., and take off hogsheads of tobacco in exchange, they might be encouraged to hold out. In fact, some of the skippers, alarmed at the threats of the patriots to burn their tobacco, actually began to trade with them. But Berkeley issued a proclamation expressly forbidding trade with the Western Shore and threatening to denounce as rebels all who disobeyed. This had the desired effect.

It was with extreme bitterness that the patriots found the merchants and masters, with many of whom they had had long and pleasant business and personal relations, leagued with the governor against them. It brought a realization that they were cut off from their native country and that there was no longer any possibility of pleading their cause before the King and the English public. When Captain Thomas Grantham arrived in a five hundred-ton ship, the *Concord*, carrying thirty-two guns and a crew of forty or fifty, Lawrence wrote him in a vain attempt to gain his sympathy. The people had been grievously oppressed and had taken up arms in their own defense, he said, so that he hoped the merchants would remain neutral. But if they insisted on aiding the governor, the planters were resolved to burn their tobacco and the ships would have to return without cargoes. Grantham replied that he would not treat with men in arms against the royal authority, and that nothing but a "speedy repentance" could save him, his friends and the country from ruin.

But though Grantham gave his support to the governor, he believed it his duty to proffer his services to both sides for a general reconciliation. Berkeley he tried to "persuade to meekness," arguing that an unrelenting temper on his part would only "harden the people in their obstinacy and render them desperate." It would have required a past master in persuasion to replace the wounded pride and the hatred in Sir William's heart with meekness, but it was not difficult to make him see the advantages of coming to terms with the patriots. Often during the past few months he must have thought with dread of the day when he would stand before the King to make his excuses for the collapse of his authority in Virginia; it would add to his shame to have this authority restored by English troops. Could he persuade the patriots to lay down their arms so that he could greet the commanders of the King's forces, not from his place of exile on the Eastern Shore or from on board his fleet in the York, but from his residence at Green Spring, he would appear in a much better light. So he authorized Grantham to open negotiations with Ingram.

Ingram was quite willing to listen to reason. He must have realized that the end was at hand and he had intimations that some of his own party were plotting to depose him from the chief command. It might be well to save his neck while there was opportunity; after the arrival of the English troops it would be too late. So he arranged a conference between Grantham and "the principal ringleaders" of his army near Pate's house. It was a strange trick of fate which placed the surrender of Bacon's little army almost at the very spot where Bacon himself had died, and one is inclined to wonder why the memory of his indomitable spirit did not inspire them to greater courage and determination. One can easily imagine the gloom, the fear, the sullen hopelessness, the anger which flitted alternately over the faces of the little group as Grantham pleaded with them.

"What, gentlemen," he said, "are you going to your ruin headlong? Are you quite bereft of all sense of duty and self-preservation? Have you not yet heard what numerous forces are coming from England to suppress your tumultuous proceedings, and that without an immediate submission your fate will be inevitable? Hearken therefore to the tenders of peace before it is too late. Consult like men of sense your own felicity and quietly lay down your arms, lest by persisting in this open hostility you force them at last to be sheathed in your own bowels."

The governor's terms were very liberal, he said. All who surrendered were to be pardoned and were to receive pay for the full time of their service since the granting of Bacon's commission. Those who so desired were to be retained in arms to fight the Indians, while indentured workers in the ranks were to be freed and their masters compensated from the public treasury. This was a tempting offer indeed for men in desperate straits, but it must have been obvious that it was an attempt to make them desert not only the cause for which they had sacrificed so much, but their comrades in other parts of the colony. George Milner, a staunch loyalist, had suggested to Grantham that he try to persuade the governor to announce a general amnesty similar to the Declaration of Breda, with which Charles II had reassured all England before his return from exile. But Berkeley's purpose was to detach the main body of troops from the patriot cause so that he would be free to proceed against the remaining leaders. As the desperate group discussed Grantham's proposals there were loud protests and some "severe threats," but in the end all gave in and promised to lay down their arms.

The chief blame for this desertion lies with Ingram. He should have come to no agreement with the governor which did not include Drummond, Lawrence and other patriot leaders and perhaps even the prisoners in Berkeley's hands. His treachery was not comparable to that of Benedict Arnold, for he bartered off the cause to which he was pledged merely for his neck, not for financial gain and high command. But there was good cause for the bitter denunciations hurled upon his name by hundreds of brave men in all parts of Virginia whom he left exposed to the fury of Berkeley's revenge. Had he not laid down his arms like a "cowardly, treacherous dog," they said, we would have gone out to meet the English troops and died at "the face of our enemies," instead of being trapped in isolated posts or hunted down in woods and swamps.

Even after the surrender of the leaders of the forces at West Point it was not certain that Bacon's veterans could be induced to follow their example. But Grantham appeared among them to tell them that peace had been concluded upon generous terms and that he had been commissioned to take them to the governor to make their submission. So they all gave up their arms and, clambering aboard one of the ships, sailed down the York to Tindal's Point. A picturesque yet sad sight it was as these veterans, never defeated on the field of battle but now deprived of their youthful leader and deserted by his successor, filed past the crabbed old governor standing on the deck of his ship, to "kiss his hand" and take the oath of allegiance.

Grantham's next move was to secure the surrender of Gregory Wakelett, who was stationed in Gloucester County with a force of cavalry. So anxious was the governor to remove this last serious obstacle to peace that he offered Wakelett not only his pardon but part of the plunder taken by Bacon from the Indians. So he too brought his force to Tindal's Point, where Grantham met him with "a considerable company of resolved men," to take over their arms and conduct them before the governor. When Captain Drew, at the strongly fortified post of Green Spring, surrendered "upon his own terms," the governor found himself in possession of almost all the populous region between the James and Rappahannock.

But he still had to reckon with his archenemies, Lawrence and Drummond. At the time of Ingram's surrender they were stationed with a small force at a place called Brick House on the south side of the York about two miles from West Point. When their desperate efforts to prevent the surrender failed, they determined to draw together the remnants of the patriot forces and retire toward the frontier. So they sent posthaste for Whaley at King's Creek and when he arrived with his garrison and the last remains of Colonel Bacon's cattle and corn, they found themselves in command of about three hundred men and boys. With these they retreated into New Kent, hoping to arouse once more the fighting spirit of the frontier region. But even here the people were tired of anarchy, so that their appeals fell on deaf ears. Their force instead of growing began to melt away, until they were entirely deserted and forced to seek safety in flight.

Lawrence, Whaley and three of their comrades made good their escape. The last report of them came from a plantation on the extreme frontier, where they were seen to disappear in the forest, armed with pistols and pushing their horses on through the snow. The fate of this little group is shrouded in mystery. They may have died of starvation in the wilderness; they may have fallen before the tomahawk of the Indians. It was whispered through the colony that they had drowned themselves in some deep river, preferring suicide to the governor's malignant cruelty.

There is some reason to think, however, that these brave men did not die at all and that they eventually reached New England, to live there in seclusion like the regicides William Goffe and Edward Whalley. In the Boston town records of July 29, 1678, we find this entry:

"William Mason, brick-layer, Charles Cleate dancing-master, Clasen Wheeler his serv't fiddler, of Virginia, all at John Smith's butcher, and p. George Joy, said to be in the rebellion of Nathaniel Bakon there." It must have been a meager income that they could earn by giving dancing lessons in Puritan Boston, but life at John Smith's the butcher was preferable to death on the gallows. We have no means of identifying these men; they may have been Lawrence's party, they may have been some other group of fugitives—possibly William West and John Turner who were condemned to death but broke out of prison and disappeared.

While Grantham was doing such stellar work for the governor in the York River, Captain Robert Morris of the ship *Young Prince* was cooperating with a group of loyalists for the subjection of the south bank of the James. We find him cruising up stream and down, conveying troops from place to place, surprising isolated garrisons, persuading some of the patriots to make their peace with the governor, capturing others and holding them prisoners on his ship. On December 29, he assisted in the storming of a fort, apparently on Warwickqueke Bay, and on January 6 he led a flotilla of three ships, one ketch and three sloops with a considerable body of troops on board up past Jamestown to stamp out the last embers of the uprising in Henrico. But the very next day he received word that Henrico "had risen for the King," so that there remained for him only to visit the governor and hand over to him fifteen or sixteen prisoners.

In the meanwhile, Berkeley, even before he set foot on the Western Shore but when final success seemed assured, proceeded to wreak vengeance on his unfortunate prisoners. It was on January 11, 1677, that a court-martial consisting of Berkeley, Ballard, Ludwell, Beverley and others of the chief loyalists, sat on the deck of Captain John Martin's ship in the York River off Tindal's Point, to convict Thomas Hall of treason and condemn him to be hanged. The next day they passed sentence on three more, Thomas Young, who had served under Cromwell in the English civil war; Henry Page, a carpenter; and James Wilson. As these brave men were rowed ashore and stood beneath the gallows on the site of Yorktown, one wonders whether an unkind fate did not vouchsafe one last favor in the form of a vision, a vision of two long lines of soldiers, those on one side in uniforms of buff and blue, on the other in white, with thousands of men in red marching in between to lay down their arms. It would have solaced the last moments of these martyrs to the cause of American liberty to know that they were meeting their fate upon the very spot where a century later that cause was to triumph. And Americans today, when they visit Yorktown to pay tribute to George Washington and the patriots of the successful revolution of 1775, should pause to do reverence also to the men who sacrificed their lives in the unsuccessful revolution of 1676.

After these executions the governor moved up the York to King's Creek and landed at Colonel Bacon's house, which he found almost completely stripped. The day of his arrival Captain Morris came up with his prisoners, among them Drummond, whom he had found hiding in Chickahominy Swamp. As the sturdy Scotsman was led before the governor there was enacted a characteristic scene of Berkeleian vindictiveness. Making a low bow the governor said: "Mr. Drummond, you are very welcome, I am more glad to see you than any man in Virginia. Mr. Drummond, you shall be hanged in half an hour."

Drummond replied: "What your honor pleases."

Perhaps Berkeley's advisers persuaded him that to carry out this threat and execute a prisoner without even a pretense of legality might bring severe criticism upon him in England, for he summoned a court-martial at Colonel Bray's house at Middle Plantation the next day to try him.

Drummond was treated with brutal harshness, his ring was torn from his finger, his clothes were taken from his back and he was kept overnight in irons on board one of the ships. The next morning he was forced to walk, still in irons and without a cloak, five miles in the sharp January weather from King's Creek to Middle Plantation. When he complained that his shackles hurt him, the guard, more merciful than Sir William, offered to let him mount a horse. This kindness he refused with the remark that he would come to his death quickly enough on foot. But he expressed gratitude for permission to rest on the roadside while he smoked a pipe. At Colonel Bray's he was brought before the governor, who had arrived in his coach, Colonel Bacon, Ludwell and several others and after a hearing of only half an hour, in which he was not permitted to say anything in his own defense, was condemned to death. Four hours later he was hurried away to his execution. Not content with this, Berkeley's malice sought out his victim's widow, to seize her plantation, take away the very contents of her house and force her with five children to flee into the woods and swamps where they nearly perished of hunger. When this matter came to the attention of the English Privy Council, the Lord Chancellor exclaimed that if it were proper to wish a dead person alive he would wish Sir William so, "to see what could be answered to such barbarity."

Nor did Berkeley's revenge stop here. With Drummond was sentenced John Baptista, a Frenchman, whom the governor declared had been "very bloody." Sir William's return to Green Spring was not calculated to move him to moderation, for he found his plantation stripped of grain and cattle, and his residence damaged from its long occupation by the troops. On January 24, James Crews, Bacon's neighbor and ardent friend, and John Digby, "from a servant made a captain," were brought before the court-martial and straightway condemned. In one of those flashes of malice which give us so clear an insight into Berkeley's character, he ordered that these two men be hanged on the site of Bacon's camp at Sandy Bay, in revenge for the humiliation he had endured there. With Crews and Digby were condemned three others, William Rookings, William West and John Turner, but Rookings cheated the hangman by dying in prison, and the other two by breaking out and escaping from the colony. Henry West was let off with a sentence of banishment and the confiscation of his estate.

It was with bitterness that the governor's friends returned to their plantations to find that their stores had been plundered, their cattle driven off, their barns emptied or burned, their servants liberated, their silver, farm implements, utensils, their very furniture carted away. Like the loyal sufferers of the English civil war who demanded restitution after the return of Charles II, they set up a clamor for compensation from the estates of the "rebels." Was it right, they said, that they should suffer for their loyalty to the King and governor, now that the authority of the King and governor had been restored? An undignified scramble ensued, marked by confiscation and illegal seizures. So far from condemning these proceedings, Sir William took the lead, showing a "greedy determination thoroughly to heal himself before he cared to staunch the bleeding gashes of the woefully lacerated country," seizing men's estates, cattle, servants and tobacco. Some men he threw into prison and forced to make over their property by threats of hanging. A certain James Barrow was locked up at Green Spring and exposed to hunger, cold and vermin until he yielded to the demand to make a ruinous payment to the governor.

Amid this orgy of hatred and revenge, it was not to be expected that mercy should be shown to the widow of the chief "rebel." We have no means of knowing what happened to Elizabeth Bacon in the three months following her husband's death. She probably remained in seclusion at Curles Neck, having for consolation the knowledge that her grief was shared not only by neighbors and friends but by the mass of the people of Virginia. Even with the final loss of the cause for which her husband gave his life she was not immediately ejected from her house, for though he was "attainted of high treason" on February 29, 1677, and all his land, "chattels, real goods, debts and other principal estate" confiscated, she was to retain possession until the King's wishes were known. Yet her position was truly pathetic. With the heroic husband to whom she was so devoted dead and stigmatized as a traitor, estranged from her own family, her inheritance cut off, awaiting the day when she would have to move out of her home, the future must have seemed black indeed. It is possible that some one of her husband's friends who had escaped Berkeley's wrath may have befriended her. Eventually she married Thomas Jarvis, of Elizabeth County, a merchant and sea captain, who owned a "trading plantation" on the site of Hampton. When he too died she married a certain Edward Mole. Of her two daughters by Nathaniel Bacon, Elizabeth died in childhood and Mary lived to marry Hugh Chamberlain of Alderton Hall, Suffolk, physician to Queen Anne.

LIBERTY DEFERRED

Late in January 1677, a small fleet came in through the capes and anchored in the mouth of the James River. On board were Sir John Berry, in command of the ships, Colonel Herbert Jeffreys, with a part of a regiment of English troops, and Colonel Francis Moryson, joint commissioner with the other two for settling the "grievances and affairs of Virginia." They announced that the frigates and the remainder of the transports with men sufficient to make up a regiment of one thousand men were following them. Four days later Berkeley came aboard to relate all the exciting events of the past few months—the forcing of a commission by Bacon, the flight to the Eastern Shore, the burning of Jamestown, the death of Bacon, the plundering of the estates of the loyal party, the final collapse of the uprising and the restoration of the governor to power. The commissioners placed in Sir William's hands a package of letters and instructions from the King and the Board of Trade and had him rowed ashore.

When Sir William read these papers he was beside himself with rage. In June 1676, he had written to the King, stating that he was old and infirm and asking to be relieved from active service. Now he found that this request had been granted. We direct you to repair to England, said the King in a personal letter, to give us an account of the present commotions in Virginia, and though you are to retain the title of governor we have appointed Herbert Jeffreys to carry on our service there. Whatever may have been Berkeley's wishes in June, at this moment he was determined to let nothing, not even his loyalty to the King, balk him in sating his thirst for revenge and in retrieving his losses. And this determination became even more fixed when Jeffreys showed him a royal proclamation which he was directed to publish, granting pardon to all concerned in the uprising with the one exception of Bacon.

There followed angry discussions on board the *Bristol* and long and earnest consultations with the councillors. Finally Berkeley announced that the word "conveniency" in his orders, gave him permission to postpone the date of his departure and the surrender of his authority as long as he wished. As for the proclamation, he refused to publish it until he had prepared one of his own to accompany it, in which he excepted from the general pardon a number of men now awaiting trial. The commissioners warned him not to trifle thus with the royal commands, but Berkeley was blind to all save his burning desire for revenge. Since there was no cable or wireless in those days by which his disobedience could be reported to the home government, he knew that he was safe from interruption. The commissioners might denounce him in their letters, but Bland and the others would be hanged as high as Haman before any reproof or further orders could reach Virginia. So the trials and executions continued.

The only concession Berkeley would make was to replace the courts-martial with civil trials. On March 3, at Green Spring, John West and Charles Scarburg, although their lives were spared, were subjected to ruinous fines for "dishonoring the governor." On March 8, the luckless Giles Bland, who had been held a prisoner for more than five months aboard the *Adam and Eve*, was brought to trial before a jury and condemned to death. With him was sentenced Robert Jones, a veteran of the royal army in the civil war. This old soldier pleaded for pardon, throwing open his clothes to show the wounds he had received in the service of Charles I. So moved was Moryson, who with Berry and Jeffreys sat on the court, that he wrote Lady Berkeley begging her to intercede with the governor for mercy. Although she replied that she would rather wear the canvas clothes the "rebels said they would make me glad of" than comply, her husband did consent to a reprieve and many months later Jones received a pardon from the King.

In quick succession other trials and hangings followed—those of Anthony Arnold, Richard Farrar, Robert Stokes, John Isles, Richard Pomfrey, John Whitson, William Scarborough. Some of these men merely bowed their heads before a cruel fate and stood in silence as they were accused and condemned, but sturdy Anthony Arnold boldly defended the right of the people to resist oppression and injustice. Kings have no rights but what they got by conquest and the sword, he said, as he stood facing Berkeley and the other judges, and he who can by force of the sword deprive them thereof has as good and just a title to them as the King himself. If the King should deny to do me right I would think no more of it to sheath my sword in his heart or bowels than of my mortal enemies. Listening with horror to these words from the "resolved rebel and traitor," the court ordered for him an execution especially humiliating. So he was taken to his own county and there hanged in chains, "to be a more remarkable example than the rest."

So bitterly angry were the people at the governor's brutality that they would have arisen in arms a second time had a leader appeared and had they not been cowed by the redcoats and the frigates. But so obvious was their sullen discontent that it was feared they might rescue some of Berkeley's victims, and his friends advised him not to send them to die without a strong guard. We have no means of knowing whether Colonel Bacon and the other members of the Council tried to stay the hand of the governor. They were so accustomed to yielding to his every wish that they probably were helpless in this crisis when a word of opposition would have enraged him. The three commissioners protested in vain and had to content themselves with writing the King that Berkeley seemed willing to risk a new uprising in order to sate his lust for revenge. As for Charles, he sent peremptory orders for Berkeley to forget his "passion or resentment" and obey his orders to come home at once. "That old fool," he remarked to his courtiers, "has hanged more men in that naked country, than I did for the murder of my father."

Knowing that his days in Virginia were brief, Berkeley made the most of his time. The Assembly which was summoned to meet on February 20, was elected amid the general terror inspired by the executions and so was packed with Berkeley's friends, his "own creatures" selected personally for election. When intimidation was not effective, the loyal party resorted to fraud. As was to be expected, these men proceeded to confirm all that Berkeley had done and passed a series of oppressive measures of their own, fining certain men, banishing others and forcing some to make submission with ropes around their necks. They passed resolutions praising the governor and exonerating him from blame for the uprising, and voted him large sums of money to recompense his losses. They snubbed the commissioners, answered the grievances of the various counties with threats of dire punishment and declared all the reforms enacted by the so-called Bacon's Assembly null and void.

When Sir William finally turned his back on Green Spring and embarked on the *Rebecca* to return to England, he left a colony still divided against itself, the mass of the people sullen and bitter. In many a humble cottage it was hoped that Lawrence might emerge from the forest to put himself at the head of the people in one last desperate battle for freedom. Some talked of the possibility of "abandoning their plantations" and retreating westward to establish a new state in the wilderness.

But Sir William, as his ship weighed anchor and slipped slowly down the James, was more concerned with what awaited him in England than with the mutinous spirit of the Virginians. And many times on the voyage across the Atlantic, pacing back and forth on deck, his clutch on the throat of his enemies at last loosened and his interview with the King approaching, he must have wondered how he could explain his failures and his disobedience. It would take all the influence of his brother, Lord John Berkeley, all his own long years of loyalty, to excuse the fact that he had driven the people of Virginia into open insurrection and had flouted the King's pardon. Worn out by his violent passions and exertions and apprehensive of the future, he fell ill on shipboard and reached England in a very critical condition. His brother received him kindly and promised his support in "clearing his innocency," and Charles sent word that he would be glad to see him as soon as he had regained his health. But fate made it unnecessary for him to make any excuses or plead his cause with his royal master, for his condition became critical and on July 13, 1677, he died. He was interred at Turchenham.

Thus eight months after the death of Bacon the other principal figure in the tragic events of 1676 was removed from the scene. Strangely enough it was Berkeley, who, after spending most of his life in Virginia, came back to England to die, while Bacon who had been in America only two years was buried in Virginia soil. Yet it was appropriate that it should be so. Berkeley remained an Englishman to the end, almost untouched by the spirit of the New World with its tendency toward individualism, equality and freedom. Bacon, on the other hand, found himself immediately at home on the frontier. There was something in his character—his hatred of injustice, his dislike of ostentation and sham—which gave this sophisticated graduate of Cambridge a kinship with the rough planters of Henrico and New Kent.

Berkeley remained to the end an English loyalist of the age of James I and Charles I, Bacon was an American patriot, akin not so much to Cromwell or Pym as to George Washington and Samuel Adams.

As we peer back through the centuries we wish that we knew more about this young man who played so important a rôle in Virginia and American history. We would welcome the discovery of his letters to his father from Holland or Italy or Henrico, telling of his interests, hopes, plans or everyday life on his tobacco plantation. We would like to know what were his first impressions of Virginia, what he thought of Jamestown, what was his estimate of his neighbors. But though much that is essential to a clear picture is missing, incidents in his life reveal certain traits with vivid clearness.

We see a man of unusual mental ability, a clear thinker and convincing debater, but impatient of the drudgery necessary to master mathematics or the classics; impulsive in maturity as in youth and not inclined to weigh the ultimate cost of hasty action; irresponsible in financial matters and apt to be extravagant; warm in his loves and his friendships; an uncompromising enemy of injustice; possessing to a remarkable degree that indefinable quality known as magnetism which drew men to him and won their confidence and affection. We know that Bacon had his faults, but they were faults which blended with his virtues to make the unusual man. Perhaps had he not got into trouble at Cambridge, or had not incurred the hostility of his sweetheart's father, or had not wasted his patrimony, he would not have placed himself at the head of the Virginia frontiersmen to go out against the Indians, or have bearded the governor at Jamestown, or have become the one great champion of American rights in the seventeenth century.

The more one examines the movement which Bacon headed, the more its kinship with the American Revolution becomes apparent, for both had as the main principle the defense of American rights. Neither Sir William Berkeley nor George III grasped the fact that Virginia was more than a part of an extended England, that the people were more Virginians than Englishmen, that they had interests apart from those of the mother country, that the isolated life upon the plantation or on the frontier made them self-reliant and impatient of restraint.

Not only were the fundamental causes of the two uprisings the same, but the course of events was similar. As it was the Sugar Act which brought distress to the merchant class in the colonies in 1764, so it was the Navigation Acts which undermined the prosperity of Virginia in the years from 1660 to 1676 and reduced the planters to poverty. As it was the Stamp Act which threatened representative government in America by wresting from the Assemblies the control of taxation, so it was Berkeley's system of corrupting the burgesses and then continuing them on indefinitely without an election which turned representative government into a farce in Virginia. As the patriots of 1775 rose first to defend their liberty, seeking independence only when they found that they could not have one without the other, so the patriots of 1676 had no thought of breaking away from the mother country until they learned that English frigates and

English redcoats were on their way across the Atlantic to suppress them. As the patriots of the Revolution sought mutual protection in a union of the colonies, so Bacon, when death cut him down, was planning a union of Virginia, Maryland and North Carolina. As Congress in 1778 was forced to seek the aid of foreign countries, so Bacon and his advisers had visions of foreign warships in Chesapeake waters and foreign troops on Virginia soil. As the Revolution was in a sense a civil war, with neighbor fighting neighbor and son turned against father, so the uprising in Virginia found class arrayed against class and to some extent section against section. The chief difference is the fact that in the later movement the repressive measures came directly from a reactionary British government, while in the earlier the chief cause of trouble was the despotism of a governor whose power was entrenched by his influence in the Privy Council.

Had Nathaniel Bacon been in Virginia during the Dutch wars, and had Indian troubles or some other event precipitated an uprising at that time, it is possible that the entire Chesapeake Bay region might have been lost to England. With Virginia, Maryland and North Carolina in arms, with Dutch merchant vessels taking off their tobacco and supplying them with weapons, ammunition and other goods in return, and with Dutch warships guarding the entrance through the capes, England might have had to yield. But alone the three colonies were helpless. They were too weak in numbers, perhaps not more than one hundred thousand souls in all, too dependent upon the supply of English goods, too exposed to attack because of their great open rivers, too disunited, too lacking in leaders.

But though the Virginia patriots were suppressed, though their heroic young leader came to an untimely death, though the liberal laws passed under his influence were annulled, though his chief supporters were led to the gallows and stigmatized as traitors and rebels, "Bacon's Rebellion" was not without its lasting influence upon American history. It put an end to the Berkeleian system of government by corruption, for there were no more long Assemblies in the colony; it brought about reform in local government since many of Bacon's laws were reenacted in later sessions; it fortified the people to resist the assault on their liberty known as the second Stuart despotism; it gave the English Privy Council a realization of what was to be expected when the Americans were driven to desperation. But after all, the movement was symptomatic rather than conclusive. The flight of Berkeley to the Eastern Shore foreshadowed the flight of Dunmore to Norfolk and Gwynn's Island; the burning of Jamestown by the patriots of 1676 had its counterpart in the burning of Norfolk by the patriots of 1776; Bacon's Declaration of the People was the forerunner of the Declaration of Independence.

Nathaniel Bacon has never received due recognition as the true seventeenth-century patriot, who gave his life in the cause of American liberty. One looks in vain for a fitting monument to him in Richmond, or at Jamestown, or in the nation's capital. Historians who speak of Samuel Adams or Patrick Henry as patriots, continue to call Bacon "the rebel," forgetting that he championed in arms the cause of freedom a century before they rang the alarm bell of liberty. We have no right to ignore his memory merely because the movement he led ended in seeming failure. Let us not forget that though the sun of American liberty sank blood red across the James as the old governor sent one patriot after another to the gallows, it was the same sun which rose a century later to shine down upon the triumph of the man we call the Father of His Country.

ESSAY ON AUTHORITIES

Essay on Authorities

ALTHOUGH THE SOURCE MATERIAL FOR THE REBELLION IN Virginia in 1676 is comparatively abundant, our information concerning Nathaniel Bacon's life prior to his migration to America is meager. We cannot be certain even of the date of his birth. Historians have always accepted January 2, 1647, as correct, but the Reverend G. F. Parsons of Snape Vicarage, Suffolk, England, informs me that the church register gives January 2, 1645. However, since the entry is squeezed in between the one above and the one below, and was obviously inserted at a later date, it is probable that the wrong year was set down. The fact that Nathaniel's mother died on January 2, 1647, suggesting that she gave her life in bringing him into the world, strengthens the claim of the traditional date. It is supported also by the "Visitation of Suffolk" in 1664 which gives Nathaniel's age as eighteen, which no doubt referred to his nearest birthday.

The kindness of the British Museum in microfilming for me the manorial records of Friston Hall and other properties belonging to Thomas Bacon, throws light upon Nathaniel's boyhood surroundings. These documents include rentals of farms, sheep walks, blacksmith shop, etc., together with a list of books in the manor house. I have been able to discover little concerning Nathaniel's career at Cambridge. W. H. S. Jones, president and historian of St. Catharine's College, writes me: "Unfortunately the college record books for the period of

Nathaniel Bacon are in many respects defective. The steward's books (if they were kept) are missing from 1640 to 1680 and we have no tutor's accounts earlier than 1676."

A search through the published letters of John Ray proved more fruitful, Robert W. T. Gunther's *Further Correspondence of John Ray*, giving us our only description of Bacon as a boy. It is to be hoped that more Ray manuscripts may be unearthed and that they will contain other letters with glimpses of Ray's young pupil and travelling companion. John Churchill's *Collection of Voyages and Travels*, although provokingly silent upon personal matters relating to Bacon—his appearance, disposition, interests and political views—permits us to follow him through the *grand tour* of Europe and to evaluate this experience as a factor in his education. But at Gray's Inn once more we are baffled, since many of the records were destroyed in the disastrous fire of 1684. We do not know even the dates of his residence, and must conjecture as to the influence of his teachers and fellow students.

A search of court records in the British Public Record Office has been more successful. The courtesy of the secretary in sending photostatic copies of the bill of complaint of the former Elizabeth Duke against her brother, Sir John Duke, the latter's answer and other important papers in the hearing before the Lord High Chancellor of England, has cleared up many important points in the matter of Bacon's marriage and his subsequent financial status. Similarly the complaint of Robert Jason before Lord Guilford against Bacon's wife and his father, published in Volumes XIV and XV of the *Virginia Magazine of History and Biography*, suggests at once the main reasons for the migration to Virginia.

ESSAY ON AUTHORITIES

The destruction of the Henrico records from the founding of the county to 1677, throws a veil over the movements of young Bacon after his arrival in Virginia. Yet the due-bill for land, cattle, etc., which he purchased of Thomas Ballard in 1674, gives the location of his plantation. Also the fact that the records are available for the period immediately following Bacon's death throws much light on the economic, social and political life of which he became a part. In the absence of most of the journals of the Council of State we know very little of his rôle in that body, but his record as a judge may be followed in outline in the *Minutes of the Council and the General Court*, edited by H. R. McIlwaine.

At Jamestown recent excavations, accompanied by a study of foundations, building materials, fragments of casements, etc., enable us to reconstruct the ancient capital. We are indebted, also, to Samuel H. Yonge's *The Site of Old "James Towne"* and Henry C. Forman's *Jamestown and St. Mary's*, for painstaking investigations of the location of houses, the character of architecture and the living habits of the people. Additional information is gleaned from the countless references to the little town in W. W. Hening's *The Statutes at Large*, the *Journals of the House of Burgesses*, in official reports to the English government and in private correspondence. If funds were available the tiny capital might be rebuilt with a degree of accuracy approaching that of colonial Williamsburg.

For the causes of discontent in Virginia in the Restoration period the sources of information are abundant, the county grievances, collected by the King's commissioners, being especially detailed. When Sir John Berry, Herbert Jeffreys and Francis Moryson reached Virginia in January 1677 with instructions to inform themselves "of all grievances in general," they set on foot an investigation in each county. Although the small farmers were still under the influence of Berkeley's savage "purge" and were trembling for their lives and property, their statements are remarkably frank. The historian hesitates to accept every accusation of fraud and embezzlement, yet the grievances leave no doubt of the main motives which actuated hundreds in taking up arms. They are to be found in the British Public Record Office, C05-1371, have now been transcribed for the Library of Congress, and some of them have been published in the *Virginia Magazine*, Vols. II and III.

Even had the people been denied the opportunity to state their case their wrongs would have been obvious from other sources—from the various relations of the rebellion itself, from letters of prominent men in Virginia to the Board of Trade, from the statements, proclamations and addresses of Bacon, from the laws set forth in Hening's *Statutes at Large*, from the county records, from pamphlets describing the effect of the trade laws, from the *Minutes of the Council and General Court*.

The most detailed and probably the most accurate account of the uprising—the Indian troubles, the defiance of Berkeley, the descent on Jamestown, Bacon's Assembly, the various campaigns, the burning of the capital, Bacon's death—is the *True Narrative of the Rise, Progress and Cessation of the Late Rebellion in Virginia*, by his Majesty's commissioners. This important document which is in the British Public Record Office, has been published in Volume IV of the *Virginia Magazine* and in *Narratives of the Insurrections*, edited by Charles M. Andrews, and reproduced for the Library of Congress. The account, although it censures Bacon for his resistance to authority, is not strongly prejudiced against the "rebels," partly no doubt because of the commissioners' sympathy with their

ESSAY ON AUTHORITIES

complaints, partly from their ill-disguised admiration for Bacon himself, and partly from their animosity to Berkeley.

Valuable because of the detailed information it gives on Bacon's Assembly, the arrest of the "rebel" and the Indian war, is Thomas Mathews' *The Beginning, Progress and Conclusion of Bacon's Rebellion* published in *Force's Tracts*, in the *Virginia Historical Register*, Vol. III, in C. M. Andrews' *Narratives of the Insurrections* and elsewhere. Mathews was an eye-witness of much of what he describes, and though nearly thirty years had elapsed when he penned his narrative, the tragic events seem to have been fresh in his memory. Equally important is the account attributed to Mrs. Ann Cotton, known as *Bacon's Proceedings* and *Ingram's Proceedings*. The rather unusual style, in which simplicity and directness is sacrificed to quaint conceits and saws, does not obscure the fact that the narrative gives us many important details not to be found elsewhere, especially concerning the course of events after Bacon's death. It has been published in the *Richmond Enquirer*, September 1804; in Peter Force's *Tracts*, and in C. M. Andrews' *Narratives of the Insurrections*.

Another account, found in the papers of Captain Nathaniel Burwell and first printed in *Massachusetts Historical Society Collection*, Second Series, Vol. I, is "A Narrative of the Indian and Civil Wars in Virginia in the Year 1675 and 1676." Still another is "Virginia's Deploured Condition," *Massachusetts Historical Society Collections*, Fourth Series, Vol. IX, pp. 162-176. In "A Review, Breviarie and Conclusion," now in the British Public Record Office, the King's commissioners give a concise outline of the uprising, valuable for the numerous dates, which make it possible for us to follow in order the rather complicated course of events. This paper has been published in John Burk's *History of Virginia*, Vol. II, pp. 250-253. *Strange Newse from Virginia*, published in London in 1677, and now very rare, is a contemporaneous account, but written by one in possession of only a few important facts. "A Description of the Fight between the English and the Indians in May 1676," gives the only detailed account of Bacon's remarkable expedition to the Roanoke River, the attack on the Susquehannocks and the battle on the Occaneechee Island. This document, now in the British Public Record Office, has been published in the *William and Mary Quarterly*, Vol. IX, pp. 1-4.

Private correspondence dealing with the rebellion is, of course, in most cases violently partisan. William Sherwood and Philip Ludwell depict Bacon's men as an ignorant rabble, minimize their successes against the Indians and denounce their coercion of the governor and the Assembly; Giles Bland, on the other hand, dwells upon the wrongs of the people, and Mrs. Bacon, writing to Nathaniel's sister, Elizabeth, depicts him as a hero and the only hope of Virginia. Despite this coloring we glean a multitude of facts from these and other letters, including one from Charles II to Governor Jeffreys, one from Francis Moryson to Thomas Ludwell, one from Berkeley to Robert Beverley, one from William Travers to Giles Cole, one from Thomas Ballard to Captain Thomas Young. Indispensable also is the correspondence of the King's commissioners with the home government and with Berkeley. Most of these letters repose in the British Public Record Office, but some appear also in the *Virginia Magazine*, the *William and Mary Quarterly*, Burk's *History of Virginia* and elsewhere.

The county records yield many facts of a local nature—the gathering of arms, powder and provisions for use in

ESSAY ON AUTHORITIES

the Indian expeditions; the plundering of the plantations of Berkeley's supporters; the hounding of Bacon's men after the collapse of their uprising. Far more facts would have been available were not so many of these old documents missing—burned, it is said, by Federal troops in the War between the States. Nonetheless we still may consult the records of Lower Norfolk, Isle of Wight, Northumberland, Surry, Gloucester, York and other counties, from which extracts concerning the rebellion have been published in *Tyler's Magazine*, the *Virginia Magazine* and the *William and Mary Quarterly*.

Historians are deeply indebted to W. W. Hening, not only for publishing his voluminous work, *Virginia Statutes at Large*, but for including in it many official reports, court proceedings and other invaluable documents. He has preserved for us the laws of the Restoration period, some of which were so obnoxious to the people, as well as Bacon's remarkable series of reforms in June 1676, passed when the angry rebels were camped on the green before the State House. In addition we find in the *Virginia Statutes at Large*, "The Proclamation of Pardon of October 10, 1676"; the "Additional Instructions to Berkeley of November 13, 1676"; the "Proclamation of October 27, 1676"; "Bacon's Submission" of June 9, 1676; the proceedings of the courts-martial on board Captain John Martin's ship in York River, at James Bray's residence and at Green Spring in 1677, and other papers of equal importance.

It was the desire of the British government to get at the bottom of the "uproars in Virginia" which preserved for us the reasons given by Bacon and his followers for taking arms. Had Berkeley remained governor we may be certain that "Bacon's Letter of June 1676," (C05-1371, pp. 241-46), his "Declaration in Virginia," (C01-37-41), and his "Appeal to the People of Accomac" would never have been placed in the hands of the Board of Trade. We may be certain, also, that it was the King's Commissioners who kept the "Complaint from Heaven," (C01-36-78) and the "Appeal of the Volunteers," (C05-1371, pp. 247-54) with their bitter criticisms of the Susquehannock siege and the conduct of the Indian war on the Virginia frontier, from being consigned to the flames. We are surprised when we find in the musty records a letter from Berkeley, the Council and burgesses, justifying the uprising and praising Bacon as a patriot, until we realize that it is the statement which the "rebel" exacted on June 25, 1676, which in reality is nothing more than Bacon's own defense of his conduct.

The story of the Susquehannock war in Maryland may be pieced together in considerable detail, not only from the accounts of Thomas Mathews, the commissioners, Mrs. Cotton and others in Virginia, but from the "Proceedings of the Council of Maryland, 1667-1688," in *Archives of Maryland*, the *Maryland Historical Magazine*, etc. Of especial interest is the diagram of the siege of the fort on the banks of the Potomac, made apparently on the spot during the operations, which I found in 1910 in the British Public Record Office. With this in hand I have been able to go to the site of the fort at Mockley Point where the Piscataway Creek joins the Potomac opposite Mount Vernon, as directly as though it had been set down on a road map. As a result of this visit Mrs. Alice L. L. Ferguson, who had already done valuable work in excavating relics of the Piscataways in the neighborhood, has uncovered parts of the fort directly on the banks of Piscataway Creek. "The shore line of the creek has changed and one side of the fort has disappeared," she writes. "It is a square stockade with bastions and the post moulds are unusually large and deep."

The location of Bacon's plantation across the James from Jones' Neck is also quite positive. Not only do the deeds describe the place with some degree of accuracy, but a part of the estate still retains the old name "Longfield." Although nothing remains of the Bacon residence, the site is indicated by a group of ancient trees, some old foundations and the elevated character of the ground. It is too much to hope that the house itself can ever be restored, but excavations would no doubt lead to interesting discoveries. That Bacon was not cheated when he purchased the property is shown by the fact that the soil is still under successful cultivation. When one stands overlooking the James on the bluff which recedes gently toward the marshy woods to the south, one can picture in fancy Elizabeth Bacon as she stood on this spot more than two and a half centuries ago, looking out to the distant forests and wondering whether her husband would ever return from his daring expedition against the savages.

To the list of primary sources for Bacon's rebellion must be added many small but important documents, most of them in the British Public Record Office, "The Petition of Sarah Bland," (C01-36-50), "The Memorial of John Knight," (C01-30-78), Sir Henry Chicheley's commission as governor of Virginia, (C01-31-13.4), "Thomas Bacon's petition to the King," (C01-37-15), "William Byrd's Relation of Bacon's Rebellion," *Virginia Magazine*, Vol. V, p. 220; "Mrs. Byrd's Relation," *William and Mary Quarterly*, Vol. IX, p. 10; "Proposals of Thomas Ludwell and Robert Smith," *Virginia Magazine*, Vol. I, pp. 432-5; "Robert Beverley's Services during the Rebellion," Hening, *Statutes at Large*, Vol. III, p. 567; "Vindications of Sir William Berkeley," John Burk's *History of Virginia*,

Vol. II, pp. 259-64; "List of Persons Excepted from the King's Pardon," (C01-39-31).

A document which throws light upon Bacon's attempt to bind the upper classes to him in the famous conference at Middle Plantation is the "Declaration of Thomas Swan and others on August 3, 1676," (C01-37-42) supplemented by the "Letter to the Sheriff of Westmoreland County," (C01-37-43). Bacon's plans for the future, his anticipated alliance with Maryland and North Carolina, his hopes of success against the redcoats, are set forth in the "Dialogue between John Goode and Nathaniel Bacon," (C05-1371, pp. 232-40). Although Goode's word is not substantiated by other witnesses, I can see no reason for rejecting it. Even though he may have colored his narrative to emphasize the telling points which he scored in the argument, the statements credited to Bacon accord well with his desperate situation.

Among the secondary sources may be listed Mary Newton Stanard, *The Story of Bacon's Rebellion*, (New York, 1907); Thomas J. Wertenbaker, *Virginia under the Stuarts*, (Princeton, 1914); Edward D. Neill, *Virginia Carolorum*, (Albany, 1886); Philip Alexander Bruce, *The Economic History of Virginia in the Seventeenth Century*, (New York, 1907) and *The Institutional History of Virginia in the Seventeenth Century*, (New York, 1910); John Fiske, *Old Virginia and her Neighbors*, (Boston, 1897); John Burk, *History of Virginia*, (Petersburg, 1804-1816); Matthew Page Andrews, *Virginia the Old Dominion*, (New York, 1937); Herbert L. Osgood, *The American Colonies in the Seventeenth Century*, (New York, 1904-1907); Lyon G. Tyler, *The Cradle of the Republic*, (Richmond, 1907).

Historians will always be grateful for the printing of masses of source material in the *Virginia Magazine of History and Biography*, the *William and Mary Quarterly* and

ESSAY ON AUTHORITIES

Tyler's Magazine. For these volumes and also for the *Virginia Historical Register*, the *Lower Norfolk County Virginia Antiquary*, W. W. Hening, *Statutes at Large* and the *Calendar of Virginia State Papers*, a splendid index in two large volumes has been prepared by Dr. E. G. Swem.

INDEX

Index

Accomac, people of neutral, 142; 144; 154; 164; expedition against, 174; 176; Bacon's appeal, 174, 222
Adam and Eve, captures Bacon, 110; 121; joins Berkeley, 154; 165; 204
Allen, Major Arthur, Ingram fortifies residence of, 185; plundered, 186
Allerton, Col. Isaac, besieges Indian fort, 79-83
Arlington, headquarters for Berkeley, 141, 142; conference at, 151; rejoicing at, 153
Arnold, Anthony, hanged in chains, 205

Bacon, Elizabeth Duke, marries Bacon, 47-49; dowry, 49; at King's Creek, 51, 52; at Curles Neck, 53, 54; fears of for Bacon, 105, 134; husband's estate confiscated, 202; remarries, 202; suit of, 216; letters of, 220
Bacon, Elizabeth Kingsmill, marriage, 6; 51; one of "white aprons," 161, 162
Bacon's Epitaph, 179, 180
Bacon, Lord Francis, at Gray's Inn, 46
Bacon, Mary, marries Hugh Chamberlain, 202
Bacon, Nathaniel, republican principles, 4; ancestry, 4; childhood, 5; 14; 15; denounces Assembly, 24, 25; skepticism of, 39; life at Cambridge, 40, 41, 42; John Ray tutors, 43; tours Europe, 43-45; takes Master's degree, 45; at Gray's Inn, 46, 47; marriage, 47, 48, 49; financial troubles, 49, 50; migrates to Virginia, 50; purchases plantations, 52, 53; quarters, 55, 56; befriends yeomen, 57, 58, 64; as tobacco planter, 58; appointed to Council, 59; visits Jamestown, 60-62; sworn to Council, 62, 63; attendance at General Court, 63, 64; ignorant of Indians, 69; hates Indians, 89, 90; his overseer murdered, 90; chosen to lead Indian expedition, 92; popular hero, 93; expedition to Occaneechee island, 94-99; visits Nottoways and Meherrins, 94, 95; at Occaneechee Island, 95-99; defeats Occaneechees, 97-99; returns to Henrico, 99; proclaimed a rebel, 104, 105; frontiersmen guard, 107, 108; vindication of, 108; elected Burgess, 109; visits Jamestown with guard, 109, 110; captured, 110; submission of, 111, 112; restored to Council, 112, 113; leaves Jamestown, 117; marches on Jamestown, 118, 119; captures Jamestown, 119; meets Berkeley on green, 120; addresses Burgesses, 121; forces reforms through Assembly, 122-124; issues commissions, 124, 125; marches out of Jamestown, 124, 125; organizes army, 125; his army at falls of James, 126; addresses troops, 128; marches on Gloucester, 129; arrests leading

229

INDEX

planters, 130; manifesto, 131, 132; calls conference of planters, 132; forces oath on, 133, 134; conversation with Goode, 135-137; reasons for failure, 138; seizes the *Rebecca*, 143; sends fleet to Chesapeake Bay, 144, 145; at falls of James, 145; expedition against Pamunkeys, 146-150; ill, 156; marches on Jamestown, 156-159; the "white aprons," 161, 162; battle of Sandy Bay, 159-165; captures Jamestown, 166; burns Jamestown, 166-168; marches to Gloucester, 168; Brent's army flees before, 169; requires new oath of fidelity, 169, 170; hangs deserter, 171, 172; moderation of, 172; administration of, 173; designs on Eastern Shore, 173, 174; appeal to Eastern Shore, 174; hopes for Maryland and Carolina aid, 175-177; death of, 177, 178; burial of, 178, 179; poem in honor of, 179, 180; children of, 202; excepted from King's pardon, 203, 204; character, 208, 209; forerunner of American Revolution, 209-212; effects of his "rebellion," 211; recognition of withheld, 211, 212; date of birth, 215; due-bill of, 217; manifestoes of, 221, 222; location of residence, 223

Bacon, Nathaniel, Sr., migrates to Virginia, 5; career, 6; 13; plantation of, 50, 51; 59; urges submission on Bacon, 111, 112; 162; residence a "rebel" fort, 185; plundered, 186; at King's Creek defeat, 191; "rebels" evacuate house of, 197; 200

Bacon's Castle, "rebels" posted at, 185

Bacon, Thomas, opposes Charles I, 4; estate, 5; withdraws son from college, 42; engages John Ray as tutor, 43; enters son at Gray's Inn, 46; settlement for Elizabeth Bacon, 49; sends son to Virginia, 50; 63; petitions for son's pardon, 134; 223

Ball, Rev. John, minister of Varina, 55

Ballard, Col. Thomas, sells Bacon plantation, 52, 53; on courtmartial, 198; letter of, 220

Ballard, Thomas, at Middle Plantation, 132; wife one of "white aprons," 161, 162

Baltimore, Lord, vetoes tobacco stint, 21; 176

Baptista, John, executed, 200

Barrow, James, mistreatment of, 202

Berkeley, Lady Frances, 32; Bacon's men threaten, 118; intercession for "rebel" asked, 204, 205

Berkeley, Lord John, 14; defends brother, 207

Berkeley, Sir William, defeats Indians, 14; character changes, 15, 16; hatred of republican principles, 16; surrenders in 1652, 16, 17; elected governor, 17; opposes Navigation acts, 19; attempts to stint tobacco, 20, 21; corrupts Burgesses, 24, 25; avarice of, 31; appeases mutinies, 33; 34; appoints Bacon to Council, 59; residence at Jamestown, 60; 61; swears Bacon to Council, 62, 63; appearance, 62, 63; dominates General Court, 63, 64; out of step with times, 65, 66; captures Opechancanough, 72; condemns murder of Indian envoys, 81; disbands forces, 84, 85; peace proposals fool, 85; conduct of Indian war, 86-88; forbids Indian expedition, 88, 89; expedition to Henrico, 103-106; proclaims Bacon rebel, 104, 105; dissolves Long Assembly, 106; returns to Green Spring, 107; proclamation of May 29, 1676, 109; paroles Bacon, 110, 111; pardons Bacon, 112; restores Bacon to Council,

230

INDEX

112, 113; overawes Assembly of 1676, 114, 115; withholds Bacon's commission, 116, 117; meets Bacon on State House green, 120; grants Bacon's commission, 121; yields to Bacon's demands, 122; prisoner of Bacon, 123; in Gloucester, 127; flees to Eastern Shore, 129; accused of tyranny, 131; raids Tindel's Point, 133, 134; sends for redcoats, 135; letters go to England, 144; captures Bacon's fleet, 151-153; recaptures Jamestown, 153-155; defeated at Sandy Bay, 163, 164; evacuates Jamestown, 165; returns to Northampton, 168; Bacon calls traitor, 170; Bacon's body hidden from, 178, 179; Eastern Shore executions, 187-189; invades Gloucester, 189-192; prohibits trade with "rebels," 193; offers terms to "rebels," 193, 194; executions at Yorktown site, 199; brutality to Drummond, 199, 200; further executions, 201; confiscations by, 201, 202; flouts King's commands, 203, 204; executions of March 1677, 204, 205; overawes Assembly, 206; returns to England, 207; death, 207; not a Virginian, 208; his "system" ended, 211

Bermuda Hundred, 10; trading at, 12; 22; 53; 54

Berry, Sir John, arrives in Virginia, 203; quarrels with Berkeley, 204; sits on court, 204, 205; investigation of "rebellion," 217, 218

Beverley, Major Robert, on Eastern Shore, 141; expeditions of in York River, 186, 187; captures garrison at Howard's house, 189; sits on court-martial, 198; 220; Services of, 223

Bland, Giles, angers Berkeley, 63, 64; punished, 64; takes the *Rebecca*, 143; commands "rebel" fleet, 144, 145; 150; captured, 152; 154; Bacon tries to exchange, 172; 173; executed, 204; letter of, 220

Bland, Sarah, *Petition*, 223

Bokenham, William, involves Bacon in swindle, 49, 50

Bottom, Peter, life in England, 8; migrates to Virginia, 9; life on frontier, 10, 11; prospers, 12, 21; trade laws impoverish, 22, 23; falls into debt, 23

Bray, James, wife of at Sandy Bay, 161, 162; Drummond tried at house of, 200; 221

Brent, George, attacks Indians, 76-78

Brent, Giles, in Pamunkey expedition, 146, 147; marches against Bacon, 166; threat to Jamestown, 167; deserted by army, 169

Bridger, Joseph, 27; 63; flees with Berkeley, 141

Bristol, discussions on, 204

Bristow, Major, challenges "rebels," 190, 191

Brunning, Samuel, tutor of Bacon, 40

Burgesses, 13; corrupted, 24, 25; new election of, 106, 107; session of 1676, 114-116; Bacon addresses, 121; urge granting commission, 120, 121; pass Bacon's laws, 123, 124

Byrd, William I, 27; trading post of, 89, 91; 94; his *Relation*, 223

Carver, Capt. William, takes the *Rebecca*, 143; commands "rebel" fleet, 144, 145; 150; duped, 151, 152; captured, 152, 153; 154; 160; 172; 173

Cattle, epidemic, 29

Chamberlaine, Thomas, at Sandy Bay Battle, 161

Charles II, proclaimed King in Virginia, 16; 17; 20; 34; considers Berkeley a fool, 66; 134; letters to from Berkeley, 144; 187; 195; 201; recalls Berkeley,

231

INDEX

203; pardon of annulled, 204; disapproves hangings, 206; ready to receive Berkeley, 207; letter of, 220
Charles City, complaints of, 28; people in arms, 91, 92, 103
Cheeseman, Major Edmund, captured, 187; death of, 188
Chicheley, Sir Henry, 63; leads Indian expedition, 84, 85; commission of, 223
Churchill, John, his *Voyages*, 216
Clough, Rev. John, Bacon courtmartials, 172
Cocke, Richard, neighbor of Bacon, 54
Cocke, Thomas, neighbor of Bacon, 54
Code, John, 176
Cole, Col. William, 112; meets Bacon, 119, 120; on Eastern Shore, 141
Commissioners, The King's, arrive in Virginia, 203; quarrel with Berkeley, 204; investigate "rebellion," 217, 218; their *True Narrative*, 218, 219; correspondence of, 220
Concord, arrives in Virginia, 193
Cookson, Capt. William, Bacon writes, 166
Cotton, Mrs. Ann, her *Bacon's Proceedings*, 219; 222
Council of State, 12; 24; Bacon appointed to, 59; functions, 59; Bacon sworn to, 62, 63; Bacon suspended from, 104; restored to, 112, 113; journals, 217
Crews, James, Bacon's neighbor, 54; 91; elected Burgess, 109; captured, 110; hanged, 201
Curles Neck, Bacon purchases, 52, 53; description of, 53, 54; 60; 90; 94; 156; location of, 223
Custis, Col. John, host to Berkeley, 141

Davis, William, in Maryland rebellion, 175; hanged, 176

Digby, John, hanged, 201
Digges, Capt. William, on Eastern Shore, 141
Doegs, murders by, 76; attacked by Virginians, 77
Dragon Swamp, Pamunkeys flee to, 105, 106; Indian raids from, 146; Bacon's expedition in, 146-150; 156; 178
Drew, Capt., posted at Green Spring, 185; surrenders, 196
Drummond, William, conference with Bacon, 110; 114; described, 131; warned, 134; flees Jamestown, 155; burns own house, 167; 177; 183; 195; flight of, 197; captured, 199; executed, 200
Duke, Sir Edward, forbids daughter to marry Bacon, 47, 48; disinherits daughter, 48, 49
Duke, Sir John, settlement with Elizabeth Bacon, 49; sued by sister, 216
Dutch wars, in Virginia waters, 30, 31, 33; 210

Eastern Shore, Berkeley flees to, 129; 134; establishes base, 141; 142; 144; 151; boats from take Bacon's fleet, 151-153; expedition from takes Jamestown, 153-155; 159; value of to Berkeley, 173; Bacon's designs on, 173, 174; his appeal to, 174; threat to from Maryland, 176; invasion from expected, 177; executions on, 187-189; 211; 222
Edmundson, William, interview with Berkeley, 16
Elizabeth, captured by Dutch, 30
Elizabeth City County, 153; 202
Eveling, Christopher, eludes Bacon, 143, 144; takes Berkeley's letters to England, 144

Farloe, Capt. George, captured by Berkeley, 174; executed, 189

INDEX

Farrar, Richard, hanged, March 1677, 205
Farrill, Capt. Hubert, killed at King's Creek, 191, 192
Ferguson, Mrs. Alice L. L., unearths Susquehannock Fort, 222, 223
Fort Henry, trading post, 73; Indian trail to, 94
Friston Hall, 4; 5; 39; 40; 42; 43; 45; 47; 49; 134; 156; manorial records of, 215

Gale, Mathew, gathers arms for Bacon, 125
Gardiner, Capt. Thomas, captures Bacon, 110; to pay Bacon £70, 121; joins Berkeley, 154
General Assembly, elects Berkeley, 17; corrupted, 24, 25; 32; 57; 59; 65; erects forts on frontier, 86, 87; dissolved, 106; session of 1676, 114-116; 123-125; passes Bacon's laws, 123, 124; of February 1677, 206
General Court, 59; condemns Giles Bland, 63, 64; minutes, 217
Gent, William, 175
Gloucester, Bacon's men in, 125; petition from, 127; people of desert Berkeley, 127; Indians raid, 145; 146; 153; Bacon in, 168, 169; militia refuse Bacon's oath, 170, 171; yield to Bacon, 172; 173; 175; Bacon dies in, 177; 184; campaign in, 190, 191; "rebels" in surrender, 196; records of, 221
Goode, John, conversation with Bacon, 135-137, 224; 175
Grantham, Capt. Thomas, arrives in Virginia, 193; secures Ingram's surrender, 193-196; secures Wakelett's surrender, 196; 197; 198
Gray's Inn, records burnt, 216
Green Spring, description, 32; Bacon camps at, 158; Ingram fortifies, 185; 194; surrendered, 196; plundered, 201; used as prison, 201, 202; trials at, March 1677, 204, 205

Hall, Thomas, tried and executed, 199
Hansford, Col. Thomas, evacuates Jamestown, 155; 183; at site of Yorktown, 185; captured, 187; executed, 187, 188
Harris, John, captured, 189
Hasleham, Giles, 175
Hawkins, Major Thomas, Bacon arrests, 125, 126; court-martialed, 172
Hen, Robert, murdered by Indians, 76
Hening, W. W., prints Bacon's laws, 122; *Statutes at Large*, 217, 221; 223
Henrico, frontier life, 10, 11, 12; Bacon purchases plantations in, 52, 53; settlement, 54; life in, 55, 56; fur trade of, 56; people rise in arms, 91, 92; Berkeley's expedition to, 103-106; Bacon returns to, 107; elects Bacon Burgess, 109; 116; Bacon returns to, 117; people march on Jamestown, 118, 119; 135; 158; rises for King, 198; missing records of, 217
Hill, Col. Edward, defeated by Indians, 73
Howard, William, "rebels" fortify residence, 186; plundered by Beverley, 189, 190

Ingram, Joseph, succeeds Bacon, 184; mans isolated posts, 185, 186; successes of in Gloucester, 190, 191; forces of disorganized, 192; negotiates with Grantham, 194, 195; surrenders, 195, 196
Isham, Henry, 91
Isle of Wight, 159; records of, 221
Isles, John, hanged, March 1677, 205

James City County, 158
James River, 10; British expedition

233

INDEX

of 1652, 16; battles in, 30, 31; description of, 53; 58; falls of, 94, 103; 106; Bacon's army at falls, 126

Jamestown, 9; Peter Bottom at, 10; defended in 1652, 16; useless houses, 27, 28; 32; 33; from James River, 53; description, 60-62; excavations, 61, 62, 217; attacked by Indians, 69, 70; Pocahontas married at, 70, 71; Bacon visits, 109, 110; captive at, 110, 112; Assembly at, 1676, 114-117; Bacon marches on, 118, 119; Bacon captures, 119; occupies, 119-124; Bacon leaves, 124, 125; 150; Berkeley recaptures, 153-155; Bacon marches on, 156-159; siege of, 159-165; Bacon captures, Sept. 19, 166; burned, 166-168; 172; 173; 178; 211

Jarvis, Thomas, marries Bacon's widow, 202

Jason, Robert, defrauded, 49, 50, 216

Jefferson, Thomas, ancestry of, 3; ignorance of Bacon's principles, 122

Jeffreys, Col. Herbert, 65; arrives in Virginia, 203; quarrels with Berkeley, 203, 204; made acting governor, 203; sits on court, 204, 205; reports on "rebellion," 217, 218; 220

Johnson, John, execution of, 189

Jones, President W.H.S., on St. Catharine's records, 215, 216

Jones, Robert, Moryson secures pardon for, 204, 205

Kemp, Col. Mathew, threatened by Bacon's men, 125

King and Queen County, 150

King William County, 146

King's Creek, plantation of Nathaniel Bacon, Sr., 50, 51

Knight, John, *Memorial*, 223

Land, frauds in, 25; large grants, 25, 26

Larimore, Capt., captured by Bacon, 143; accompanies "rebel" fleet, 144; betrays fleet to Berkeley, 151-153

Lawrence, Richard, residence of, 60, 61; Bacon visits, 110; 114; house of searched, 117; character and views, 130, 131; flees Jamestown, 155; burns own house, 167; 169; 177; 183; pleads with Grantham, 193; 195; flight of, 197; fate of, 198; people hope for return of, 206, 207

Lee, Col. Richard, Bacon arrests, 130

Lightfoot, Philip, Bacon arrests, 130; at Middle Plantation, 132

Longfield, see Curles Neck

Ludwell, Philip, houses of, 60; account of Occaneechee battle, 97; flees to Eastern Shore, 141; captures Bacon's fleet, 151, 152; takes four sloops, 154; sits on court-martial, 198; 200; letter of, 220

Ludwell, Thomas, on poverty in Virginia, 18; praises Berkeley, 24; 220; *Proposals* of, 223

Mannikins, betray Susquehannocks, 96; Bacon's men accuse of murders, 97; in Occaneechee battle, 97-99

Manufactures, futile attempts, 28

Maryland, tobacco stint, 20, 21; alliance with Susquehannocks, 74, 75; give Susquehannocks refuge, 75, 76; murders in, 76; Virginians invade, 76-78; forces besiege Susquehannock fort, 78-83; 85; 173; Bacon's designs on, 175; uprising in, 175, 176; 210

Mason, Col. George, attacks Indians, 76-78

Mathews, Thomas, at Assembly, 1676, 114; draws up Bacon's commissions, 124; 130; warns Drummond, 134; his account of Bacon's Rebellion, 219, 222

234

INDEX

Meherrins, Bacon visits, 94, 95
Merchants Hope, 53; armed frontiersmen meet at, 91, 92
Middle Plantation, troops assemble at, 103; Bacon's headquarters at, 130; conference at, 132-134; Drummond tried at, 200
Middlesex County, 146; 153; 169; campaign in, 189, 190
Milner, George, suggests amnesty, 195
Milner, Thomas, at Middle Plantation, 132
Morris, Capt. Robert, campaign of in James River, 198; brings prisoners to Berkeley, 199
Moryson, Col. Francis, Bacon at plantation of, 159; King's commissioner, 203; quarrels with Berkeley, 204; intercedes for "rebel," 204, 205; reports on "rebellion," 217, 218; letter of, 220

Navigation Acts, passed, 17, 18; effects of, 18, 19
New Kent, riots in, 33; Bacon in, 94; 116; Bacon's march through, 157; 172; fails to rise for "rebels," 197
North Carolina, tobacco stint, 20, 21; Bacon hopes for aid from, 176; uprising in, 176, 177; 210
Northampton, Berkeley in, 141; 144; 154; Berkeley returns to, 168; 173; invaded, 174; 176
Northumberland, 153; 166; records of, 221
Notley, Thomas, defeats Maryland "rebels," 176
Nottoways, Bacon visits, 94, 95

Occaneechee Island, trading post, 93, 94; description, 95, 96; battle on, 97-99; 220
Occaneechees, trade of, 93, 94; aid Bacon, 95, 96; battle with Bacon, 97-99; 145; 148
Old Point, 155; 168; 192

Opechancanough, 14; massacres of, 71, 72; murdered, 72

Page, Henry, executed, 199
Page, John, at Middle Plantation conference, 132; wife of captured, 161, 162
Pamunkey Queen, flees to Dragon Swamp, 105, 106; before House of Burgesses, 115, 116; flees from Bacon, 148; escapes, 150
Pamunkeys, defeated, 71, 72; peace with, 72, 73; "foreign" Indians defeat, 73; 85; retreat to Dragon Swamp, 105, 106; treachery of, 146; Bacon's expedition against, 146-150; defeated, 150
Parsons, Rev. G. F., on date of Bacon's birth, 215
Pate, John, 175; hanged in Maryland, 176
Pate, Major Thomas, Bacon dies at house of, 177; 194
Persicles, see Rossechy
Phesant, Peter, involves Bacon in swindle, 49, 50
Piscataways, 78; fort of, 79
Pocahontas, marries John Rolfe, 70, 71
Pomfrey, Richard, hanged, March 1677, 205
Powhatan, power of, 70
Presley, William, 115

Rappahannock County, Indian raids in, 83, 84; forts in, 87; 116; Brent's army in, 169, 172
Ray, John, career of, 42; at Friston Hall, 43; tours Europe with Bacon, 43-45; correspondence of 216
Rebecca, captured by Bacon, 143; heads "rebel" fleet, 144; captured by Ludwell, 152; 154; 155; 165; 173; Berkeley sails on, 206
Rolfe, John, marries Pocahontas, 70, 71
Rookings, Major William, posted at Bacon's Castle, 185; death of, 201

235

INDEX

Rossechy, Occaneechee chief, 93; captures Susquehannock fort, 96; breaks with Bacon, 97, 98; death of, 98

St. Catharine's Hall, Bacon enters, 40; Bacon leaves, 42; Bacon returns to, 45
Sandy Bay, Bacon's army at, 159; battle at, 159-165; 166; executions at, 201
Scarborough, William, hanged, 205
Scarburg, Charles, fined, 204
Sherwood, William, residence of, 61; letter of, 220
Skewon, Capt. Edward, Bacon writes, 166
Skippon, Philip, tours Europe with Bacon, 43-45
Smith, Lawrence, 27; Bacon arrests, 125, 126; campaign against Ingram, 190, 191
Spencer, Col., meets Bacon, 119, 120
State House, 53; 60; description, 62; 110; 112; session of Assembly in, 114-116; Bacon's men before, 119-121; burnt, 167
Stokes, Robert, hanged, March 1677, 205
Surry, 159; records of, 221
Susquehannocks, warlike character, 74; defeated by Senecas, 75; retreat to Potomac, 76; murders by, 76; attacked by Virginians, 77; fort of beseiged, 78-83; "great men" murdered, 79-81; raid Virginia frontier, 83, 84, 86; peace proposals, 85; renewed raids of, 87-91; retreat to Roanoke River, 93; defeated, 96; 145; 220; records concerning, 222; fort of unearthed, 222, 223
Swann, Col. Thomas, 63; "Declaration" of, 224
Swem, Dr. E. G., index of Virginia history, 224, 225

Taxation, reforms in, 14, 15; oppressive in Virginia, 25; 26; causes riots, 1674, 33; 57; Bacon's men to stop, 119, 120
Thorpe, Capt. Otho, conference at residence of, 132; wife of one of "white aprons," 161, 162; plundered, 186
Tindal's Point, arms taken from fort, 133, 134; 145; Bacon at, 168; "rebel" submission at, 196; trials off, 199
Tobacco, low price of, 18; 22, 23, 56; attempts to curtail crops, 20, 21; cultivation, 58
Tobacco trade, restrictions on, 18, 19; 34
Tottopottomoi, killed in battle, 73; 105; 115
Trueman, Major Thomas, besieges Indian fort, 79-83; murders Indian envoys, 79-81; impeached, 81
Turkey Island, 53
Turner, John, escapes from prison, 201

Varina, 10; description of, 54, 55

Wadding, Rev. James, refuses Bacon's oath, 171; ministers at Bacon's death, 177; recruits forces for Berkeley, 190
Wakelett, Gregory, invades Middlesex, 190; surrenders, 196
Warner, Col. Augustine, Bacon at house of, 168, 169; plundered, 186
Warner Hall, Bacon's headquarters, 168, 169
Washington, Col. John, besieges Indian fort, 79-83; not guilty of murdering envoys, 81; house fortified by "rebels," 186
West, Col. John, court-martialed, 172
West, Henry, banished, 201
West, John, fined, 204
West, William, escapes from prison, 201

INDEX

Westmoreland, 166
West Point, 177; Ingram's headquarters at, 184; 186; 190; 191; troops at surrender, 196; 197
Weyenoakes, 73
Whaley, Thomas, posted at King's Creek, 185; flight of, 197; fate of, 197, 198
Whitson, John, hanged, 205
Wilford, Capt. Thomas, captured, 187; executed, 188
Wilkenson, James, Bacon hangs, 171, 172
Willughby, Francis, tours Europe with Bacon, 43-45
Wilson, James, executed, 199

Wood, Abraham, discovers Indian trail, 94
Wormeley, Ralph, on Eastern Shore, 141

Yeomen, migrate to Virginia, 8; in Virginia, 12, 13, 14; prosperity wanes, 17; oppressions of, 25-28; threaten mutiny, 32-34; struggle for survival, 34; 39; Bacon sympathizes with, 64, 65
York County, forces gather, 119; 184; records of, 221
Young Prince, in James River campaign, 198
Young, Thomas, executed, 199; letter to, 220